EIGHT WAYS TO
OVERCOME ADVERSITY

D1173130

EIGHT WAYS TO OVERCOME ADVERSITY

by

Joyce Meyer

Harrison House

Tulsa, Oklahoma

Eight Ways to Overcome Adversity
ISBN 1-57794-545-X
Formerly ISBN 1-57794-471-2
Copyright © 2002 by Joyce Meyer
Life In The Word, Inc.
P. O. Box 655
Fenton, Missouri 63026

Published by Harrison House, Inc.
P. O. Box 35035
Tulsa, Oklahoma 74153

05 04 03 02   15 14 13 12 11 10 9 8 7 6 5 4 3 2

Contents

Introduction 7

Part 1: It's All about Doing

1 Possessing the Land 15

2 Do You Really Want to Get Well? 23

3 Be a Doer, Not Just a Hearer 37

Part 2: Eight Ways to Overcome Adversity

Introduction 59

4 Remain Peaceful in the Storm 63

5 Spend Time with God 81

6 Watch Your Mouth 95

7 Submit Yourself to God 117

8 Walk in Love 137

9 Know the Difference between
Your "Who" and Your "Do" 151

10 Think About What You Are Thinking About 159

11 Pray at All Times 165

Conclusion 171

Prayers

For Overcoming Adversity 173

For a Personal Relationship with the Lord 181

Endnotes 183

Introduction

From the beginning of time, God had a good plan for our lives,[1] but His original plan was messed up by the devil, who caused the fall of man in the Garden of Eden.[2] God had given Adam and Eve dominion over everything in the Garden. But when they disobeyed God, they lost their authority, and suddenly Satan had the upper hand.

We must never forget that Satan is a thief and a liar.[3] Right from the beginning he has sought to divert the good things that are ours, and he will continue to do that if we allow him to. He will stay on our property if we don't run him off.

I thought for years that resisting the devil only meant I should take some sort of determined stand against him, that if I stood and rebuked him long enough and loud enough, he would eventually have to leave me alone. However, I discovered that this was not reality. So I sought God for the answer to my lack of victory in this area, and He showed me how to fight the enemy in a new way. I will be sharing what I learned with you in this book.

We can have dominion over the works of the devil.

God's Son Jesus came to earth and delivered us from the power and authority of the enemy. Christ is the Head of the church, and we are His body. We need to arise and take our rightful place in Him.

Jesus is seated in the heavenlies, and according to Ephesians 2:6, we are seated with Him by virtue of our faith in Him. Where He is, we are — and this is where the Bible says that He is:

Far above all rule and authority and power and dominion and every name that is named [above every title that can be conferred], not only in this age and in this world, but also in the age and the world which are to come.

And He has put all things under His feet and has appointed Him the universal and supreme Head of the church [a headship exercised throughout the church].

EPHESIANS 1:21,22

Jesus is Lord over all, and *He has put all things under His feet.* Since we are in Him, that means that the only place Satan has in our life is under our feet. Therefore, the devil has no real power or authority over us except what we give him and what he gets from us through deception.

One of his major goals is to deceive us.[4] Remember, he is a liar. He hopes we will believe his lies because if we do, then we will be deceived. Every time he deceives us, we give him the right to use his power against us.

The truth is that Satan may attack us with adversity, but he does not have to defeat us.

I have written this book so that if you have been deceived by Satan's lies in the past, you will now have knowledge of your God-given authority to walk all over him[5] — and you'll be able to exercise that authority.

Exercise Your Authority

You may think that because you are a believer, you can reach a place where the devil won't bother you anymore, but I believe that he regularly launches different attacks against us. The good news is that we are stronger than him because we have the Greater One living inside of us.

First John 4:4 says that greater is He Who is in us than he who is in the world. We are taught in Romans 8:11 that the same Spirit Who raised Christ from the dead dwells in us. As believers, we have everything we need to lead a victorious life if we will not allow the enemy to rule us.

Now when I say that we are not to allow the enemy to rule us, it does not mean that we will never have a problem. But it does mean that even in the midst of our problems we can still be joyful.

Let me ask you a question. Which is greater: to have joy because we have no problems or to have joy in the midst of our problems? Unbelievers can have joy if they have no problems, but it takes the power of the Holy Spirit to keep our joy[6] in the midst of a problem, even a big problem.

No matter what is going on in your life on the outside, if you have joy on the inside, you can still enjoy your life.

It is easy to be joyful when you understand that Satan has no right to do anything to you unjustly.

This book contains important information that the devil hopes you will never find out because you are going to gain new knowledge to help you fight him and win.

Part 1 discusses things that are important for us to do to obtain the good things God has for us and stop the devil from diverting them away from us. Part 2 covers eight ways to resist the devil and overcome his adversity. Satan cannot defeat an obedient believer who has a solid understanding of how to stand against his attacks.

You may be facing some kind of attack from the enemy right now. I pray that this message will help you to start getting *on* the attack instead of being *under* the attack because that is the key to keeping adversity from ruling your life.

Part 1:

It's All about Doing

1

POSSESSING THE LAND

Behold, I have set the land before you; go in and take possession of the land which the Lord swore to your fathers, to Abraham, to Isaac, and to Jacob, to give to them and to their descendants after them.

DEUTERONOMY 1:8

When God brought the Israelites out of Egypt after 430 years of Egyptian bondage,[1] He eventually led them to the Jordan River.[2] Just across the river was Canaan, the land He had promised to give to them and to their descendants after them. Through Moses, who was chosen by God as their leader, the Lord instructed them to go in and take possession of the Promised Land.[3]

Because of what Jesus has done for us on the cross,[4] you and I can possess the land God has given to us. We can have what He speaks of in His Word. We can live in the reality of His promises to us.

We don't have to just dream about the promises of God, talk about them and watch everybody else have them; we can actually live in righteousness, peace and joy, prosperity, healing, social and spiritual success and enjoyment of life. We can hear from God and receive the revelation knowledge He gives. We can receive godly wisdom about what we should do and the decisions we should make.

God has lots of good things stored up for His people — but in order to receive them, we must *do* something. In order to live in the good land He has set aside for us, we must be willing to go in and take possession of it.

No More Excuses

Caleb quieted the people before Moses, and said, Let us go up at once and possess it; we are well able to conquer it.

But his fellow scouts said, We are not able to go up against the people [of Canaan], for they are stronger than we are.

NUMBERS 13:30,31

Possessing the land involves dispossessing the current occupants. To the Israelites, the current occupants were Canaanites; to us, they are spiritual beings.[5]

Our spiritual enemy, Satan, seeks to divert the good things that are ours. So in order to possess the land and enjoy the many blessings available to God's children, we need to learn how to deal with the devil.

We cannot fight him through ordinary means. He is a spirit, and we must combat him with "spiritual" warfare (which we will discuss later on). We cannot be lazy or full of excuses or irresponsible and ever deal successfully with him.

That means no more excuses because an excuse is just a reason stuffed with a lie.

Each one of us has an invisible excuse bag. We carry it with us wherever we go. When God puts something on our heart to do that we don't want to do, we just reach in that bag and draw out an excuse, such as, "I'm afraid."

Just like the Israelites in Numbers chapter 13, we think that kind of excuse relieves us of our responsibility to do what God has told us to do. But God's answer to us is, "Then do it afraid!"

Who said that you cannot do what God has told you to do, even if you have to do it afraid?

Sometimes God will tell us not to do something. He may say, "I don't want you to see that movie," or "I don't want you to go to that party." When that happens, we look in our excuse bag and say, "But, Lord, everybody else is doing it." That doesn't mean you and I can do it. The whole world can do it, but that doesn't mean that we can.

We have to realize that we are individuals before God, and He is not going to ask us to be like someone else and do something or not do something just because they're doing it or not doing it. God requires us to do what is right *for us*.

Doing Our Part

For we are fellow workmen (joint promoters, laborers together) with and for God. . . .

1 CORINTHIANS 3:9

Suppose we are acting badly, just being grouchy and grumpy and treating everybody unkindly, and someone says to us, "What is your problem today?"

"Well," we may say, "I had a bad day at the office."

That is no excuse to be unkind. Many people have a bad day and still manage to be kind to others.

I don't think we have any concept of how many excuses we make that we think excuse us. But excuses don't excuse us; they only put off the inevitable.

The Promised Land is always available, but in order to live as God intends for us to live, we must do our part — not God's part, but our part.

There is a part that God does, but there is a part that only we can *do*. I am emphasizing that we must *do* on purpose. When God tells us to do something, it doesn't matter what we think about it, how we feel about it or whether we want to do it.

We all want, think and feel. But many times what God wants, what He thinks and what He feels are totally opposite of what we want, think and feel — and guess Who needs to win the battle? God does!

Spirit Versus Flesh

For the desires of the flesh are opposed to the [Holy] Spirit, and the [desires of the] Spirit are opposed to the flesh (godless human nature); for these are antagonistic to each other [continually withstanding and in conflict with each other], so that you are not free but are prevented from doing what you desire to do.

GALATIANS 5:17

This Scripture describes how the spirit wars against the flesh and the flesh wars against the spirit, how they are continually antagonistic toward each other. We must learn to deal with our own flesh and not let it rule us.

The flesh must habitually be put to death.[6] The death I'm referring to is spiritual death, rather than physical death. Spiritual death requires being empty of the world and all its ways, selfishness, self-will and all the works of the flesh.

When the apostle Paul said, *I die daily*,[7] he meant that every day he had to say no to wrong things that would hinder him from walking in the good plan God wants to release in His children's lives.

You will read more about this subject later on, but for now remember this: Many times we have major problems in our life simply because we won't get up and do what we need to do.

2

DO YOU REALLY WANT TO GET WELL?

Later on there was a Jewish festival (feast) for which Jesus went up to Jerusalem.

Now there is in Jerusalem a pool near the Sheep Gate. This pool in the Hebrew is called Bethesda, having five porches (alcoves, colonnades, doorways).

In these lay a great number of sick folk — some blind, some crippled, and some paralyzed (shriveled up) — waiting for the bubbling up of the water.

For an angel of the Lord went down at appointed seasons into the pool and moved and stirred up the water; whoever then first, after the stirring up of the water, stepped in was cured of whatever disease with which he was afflicted.

There was a certain man there who had suffered with a deep-seated and lingering disorder for thirty-eight years.

JOHN 5:1-5

I love this Scripture passage. I get so much out of this story of the man who had lain by the pool of Bethesda for thirty-eight years, waiting for the angel to come and stir up the water so he could get in and get healed of his *deep-seated and lingering disorder.*

Do you know anything about a *deep-seated and lingering disorder?* Have you perhaps been suffering from one yourself?

We know how loving Jesus was and how compassionate He was and how much He wanted to help people. He hasn't changed,[1] and He is asking us the same question He asked the man at the pool of Bethesda.

"Do You Want to Become Well?"

When Jesus noticed him lying there [helpless], knowing that he had already been a long time in that condition, He said to him, Do you want to become well? [Are you really in earnest about getting well?]

John 5:6

I believe that the Lord is saying to us in this verse, "Do you really want to possess the land? Do you really want to overcome adversity? Are you really ready to do whatever it takes to see it happen?"

We all have wants — and plenty of them. But if we really want something bad enough, then we will do whatever it takes to get it.

I got to a point in my life where I just could not stand to be upset anymore. I rebuked demons. I prayed for peace. I tried to get everybody around me to change and give me what I wanted so I could be peaceful. But none of that was working.

Finally, I just humbled myself before God and said, "Lord, I have got to have peace. I don't care what I have to do. I don't care what kind of changes I have to make. I don't care how You have to change me or how I have to adapt and adjust to everybody around me. I just have to have peace."

Now I have peace in my life, but there were certain things I had to do to get that peace. For example, I had to learn not to argue with my husband. I had to learn that when God said, "Give something away," I had to give it away. In short, I had to learn to do whatever God told me to do in my heart and in the Word.

Radical and Outrageous Obedience

And all these blessings shall come upon you and overtake you if you heed the voice of the Lord your God.
DEUTERONOMY 28:2

The promises of God don't always come without conditions. Of course, salvation comes strictly as a free gift. God does bless us. He is merciful, and He does do certain things for us that we don't deserve. Even when we haven't behaved right, we can still pray for mercy and ask God to help us.

But anybody who wants to live in the radical, outrageous, chase-you-down-the-street-and-overtake-you blessings of God has to do something to receive them.

We must realize that the blessing package described in Deuteronomy 28:1-14 is conditional. Verse 1 of that passage reads: *If you will listen diligently to the voice of the Lord your God, being watchful to do all His commandments which I command you this day, the Lord your God will set you high above all the nations of the earth.*

Then, as we have seen, verse 2 says, *And all these blessings shall come upon you and overtake you if you heed the voice of the Lord your God.*

While we want all the blessings listed in that chapter, many times we aren't willing to do what it takes to receive them.

Radical and outrageous blessings come from radical and outrageous obedience. They come from a willingness to obey God whether He tells us to do something in our heart or in His Word.

We really don't need to whine and complain about doing what God tells us to do because anything that He tells us to do, He gives us the ability to do.

"But I Can't!"

The invalid answered, Sir, I have nobody when the water is moving to put me into the pool. . . .

JOHN 5:7

This is one of the big excuses we have in our excuse bag: "I can't."

But if God says we can, we can. Remember, if God tells us to do something, He will give us the ability to do it.

"But It's So Hard!"

. . . but while I am trying to come [into it] myself, somebody else steps down ahead of me.

JOHN 5:7

Another excuse we make is, "It's too hard; it's just too hard." Every time we say that, it gets a little bit harder.

Instead of saying, "It's too hard," we need to say, "I can do all things through Christ Who strengthens me."[2]

Jesus said to this man in John chapter 5, "Do you really want to get well?" We need to ask ourselves that same question about every problem we face.

If we are struggling with this question, it may be because God has already told us the things we need to do to get our life in order and to receive the radical blessings He wants to start manifesting in our life. The problem may be that we just haven't yet done what He has told us to do.

If so, it is probably because it looks like what He has told us to do is going to be hard. It looks like it is going to be uncomfortable. It looks like we may have to put up with a few people we don't want to put up with or go somewhere we don't want to go. We may have to stay home a few nights and not run around with the crowd that may be poisoning our life anyway.

It is hard to be lonely. But there is nothing harder than being miserable all the time. If we continue to make excuses, we will have the pain that disobedience causes, and it is a type of pain that never really goes away; it's always there. There is also a kind of pain that we go through for a while that crucifies our flesh, but it brings us out of bondage into an area of glorious freedom and liberty.

It was hard for me to learn how to submit to my husband, as the Bible teaches.[3] My flesh screamed and kicked and yelled because I couldn't have my own way, and I thought I would die. But because I learned how to crucify my flesh, now our relationship is very wonderful. When my husband tells me to do something I don't want to do, or when I want to do something and he says, "No, we're not going to do that," it is so liberating not to have to spend three weeks mad and upset and having a fit. Now I have a peaceful, calm attitude of "God, I'll do whatever he wants."

It is not easy on my flesh to do that, but I would rather give in peacefully and trust God to change my husband's heart if he is wrong than to stay upset and angry and lose my peace.

If we have rebellion in our soul, we're going to have to go through some things to get rid of it. We're going to have to do what God says to do, not feed our flesh by giving in to it and doing what we feel like doing. If we deny our flesh long enough, eventually it will begin to wither and die so that it has no strength and power over us.[4]

Walk in Obedience

And those who belong to Christ Jesus (the Messiah) have crucified the flesh (the godless human nature) with its passions and appetites and desires.

GALATIANS 5:24

In the Old Testament, the male children had to go through the ritual of circumcision as a sign that they were willing to come into covenant with God.[5] That was their part: They had to be circumcised.

We still have to be circumcised today, but now God wants our hearts[6] and our flesh — our own ways of being and doing — to be circumcised to the point that we will walk in obedience to Him.

To circumcise is to cut off, or to cut back, the flesh. We do that in the spiritual sense by immediately cutting off any wrong thought or attitude that comes to our mind so our heart is right before God. We could say that the flesh has to be broken.

I believe that breaking the flesh is what the story in the Bible of the woman with the alabaster box is about. She broke that box so the expensive perfume could be poured out. In the same way, we have to break our flesh so the good things of God will pour out of us.

Pour Out the Good Things of God

And being in Bethany in the house of Simon the leper, as he [Jesus] sat at meat, there came a woman having an alabaster box of ointment of spikenard [perfume] very precious; and she brake the box, and poured it on his head.

MARK 14:3 KJV

We all have sweet perfume in us. But our alabaster box (our flesh) has to be broken so the perfume (the good things of God) can pour out of us. We are "pregnant" with the good things of God. We each have the fruit of the Spirit — love, joy, peace, patience, gentleness, goodness, faith, meekness and temperance.[7] But many times our alabaster box (our flesh) keeps them from being poured out.

Oh, but we love our alabaster box. We don't want to break it because, after all, it is such a pretty little box. We spend so much time taking care of it; we don't want it to be broken. Unfortunately, we worry too much about our comfort right now and not enough about later on.

In my ministry I love to get hold of people who are ready to make an investment now for what it will do for them later on.

"I'm Not Staying Like This!"

The invalid answered, Sir, I have nobody when the water is moving to put me into the pool; but while I am trying to come [into it] myself, somebody else steps down ahead of me.

JOHN 5:7

I love that verse. Talk about excuses: "I have nobody to do it for me, and every time I try, somebody else always gets ahead of me."

I would think that after thirty-eight years a diligent, determined person could have crawled over to the edge of that pool. Even if that man had only moved an inch a year, it seems that in thirty-eight years, he ought to have been able to get close enough to the edge to just roll over into the water when it was stirred up.

Thirty-eight years is a long time to lie somewhere, waiting for somebody to do something for you. I would have been on the edge of that pool, and next year when the angel came around, when that water started bubbling, I would have fallen in and said, "Either I'm going to get healed or I'm going to die, but I'm not staying like this."

Doing Brings Change

Jesus said to him, Get up! Pick up your bed (sleeping pad) and walk!

Instantly the man became well and recovered his strength and picked up his bed and walked. . . .

John 5:8,9

Notice that Jesus didn't say, "Oh, you poor man, I feel so sorry for you." He said, *Get up! Pick up your bed . . . and walk!*

"Get Up and Get Going"

After the death of Moses the servant of the Lord, the Lord said to Joshua son of Nun, Moses' minister,

Moses My servant is dead. So now arise [take his place], go over this Jordan, you and all this people, into the land which I am giving to them, the Israelites.

Every place upon which the sole of your foot shall tread, that have I given to you, as I promised Moses.

JOSHUA 1:1-3

God has already determined for you and me to be blessed, but as we have seen, we have got to drive out the current occupants who are sitting on our possessions, namely the enemy, in whatever form he manifests in our life.

Joshua and the Israelites had to drive out the current occupants before they could possess the land God had given to them. First they had to do something. Notice in verse 2 above that the Lord told Joshua to arise and go. In other words, "Get up and get going."

Perhaps more than ever before the church needs to get up and get going! We need to stop sitting around and waiting for some pool to bubble up. We need to quit wanting everything to happen by a miracle.

Please don't misunderstand me. I believe in miracles, and I praise God for them. But I get tired of hearing people say, "When am I going to get my miracle?"

You and I have got a miracle if we are saved. We have got another miracle if we are filled with the Holy Spirit. We live in miracles every day. We have miracles, but God does not always deliver us from everything by miraculous means. Sometimes He does, but sometimes He doesn't.

Sometimes we have to go through. Sometimes we have to get up, get going and just keep moving forward.

3

Be a Doer, Not Just a Hearer

This Book of the Law shall not depart out of your mouth, but you shall meditate on it day and night, that you may observe and do according to all that is written in it. For then you shall make your way prosperous, and then you shall deal wisely and have good success.

Joshua 1:8

This verse is just one of several I would like for us to consider in this chapter. All the verses that we will examine discuss being a doer of the Word.

In this verse, *do* is probably the most important word. We make a big deal out of meditating on (thinking about) the Word of God. Why? So we can do it. *For then,* the verse says, we will make our way prosperous; *For then* we will deal wisely; *For then* we will *have good success.*

When is *then?* It is after we have done what the Word of God tells us to do.

One thing the Word clearly tells us is that we cannot expect to have prosperity if we don't tithe because by refusing to pay our tithe, we are robbing God.[1] It doesn't matter what we think about tithing. It doesn't matter whether or not we want to tithe. It doesn't matter whether or not we feel like tithing. That is what God has said we are to do if we want to be blessed.

A lack of doing is a roadblock to the blessed life God has planned for us. In Malachi 3:10,11 He tells us, in essence, "If you bring all the tithes and offerings into the storehouse (the places from which you are being fed), I will rebuke the devourer for your sake."

We are settling for less when we try to rationalize our way out of tithing or doing anything else

God asks us to do, or when we say we believe it, but we don't do it.

Believe It and Do It

These people draw near Me with their mouths and honor Me with their lips, but their hearts hold off and are far away from Me.

MATTHEW 15:8

It is interesting how many people *say* they believe something, but really their belief is nothing but mental assent.

"I believe in tithing," they say. But they don't really believe because if they did, they would be tithers.

If we don't do it, then we don't believe it.

I know there are situations in which a person may be married to someone who won't let them tithe. I am not talking about that. God knows our heart, and He knows what we can do and what we cannot do. But if we are serious about tithing, even if we are married to somebody who says, "You're not tithing off my income," we will find some way to give. We can believe God for seed. But if we do that, when God puts the seed in our hands, we have to be sure we use it as seed.

Many times we say, "Lord, if I had $100, I would give it to You." Then God gives us $100, and we go out and buy a new outfit with it. What we need to do is use that $100 as seed. Then God may give us $1,000 in return.

"How will He do that?"

I don't know. The principles of the kingdom of God don't make any sense according to the principles of the world's system. But God has all kinds of ways to bless us.

The Difference Is Doing

What do you think? There was a man who had two sons. He came to the first and said, Son, go and work today in the vineyard.

And he answered, I will not; but afterward he changed his mind and went.

Then the man came to the second and said the same [thing]. And he replied, I will [go], sir; but he did not go.

Which of the two did the will of the father? They replied, The first one. . . .

MATTHEW 21:28-31

I remember a woman who attended one of my conferences. It was a banquet, and the people who attended were sitting at tables together having a meal.

This woman was sitting with a group of ladies. At the end of the conference she came to me and said, "You know, I really learned a lesson this weekend."

"What's that?" I asked.

She said, "As I listened to all those ladies talk about their problems and their breakthroughs, about what God has done for them, where they came from and where they are now, I realized that many of them have gone through the same thing I went through, which was abuse in childhood."

Then she said, "Every single thing that God has spoken to those ladies, He has spoken to me over the years. Everything that He has told them to do, He has also told me to do. The only difference is, they did it, and I didn't."

The woman received a great revelation that day. She realized that she was no different than anyone else, that her problems were no worse than many other people's. What she needed to do was begin doing what God told her to do. Then she would have the same victories that other obedient people were experiencing.

The devil tries to convince us that we are different from everybody else so that we keep asking, "Why is everybody else getting their breakthrough, and I'm not?"

Now God delivers people at different times — it may be soon, or it may take some time. We must leave that to God because our times are in His hands.[2] But it is also possible that God has told us the same thing He has told those who have received a breakthrough. The difference may simply be that they have done what He said, and we haven't.

We get all excited when God tells us about receiving the blessing, but our flesh doesn't get excited at all about the *doing* part of receiving that blessing.

We are going to be doing something anyway. All God is asking us to do is what He says and not what we want or feel like.

Do the works of God, not the works of the flesh. Activity birthed out of the flesh will prevent us from living in His blessings.

Blessing Follows Doing

If you know these things, blessed and happy and to be envied are you if you practice them [if you act accordingly and really do them].

JOHN 13:17

What a profound mystery that Christ came as a servant to us, yet we find it hard to serve others. In this verse, He gives us an awesome example of how we should serve one another, even, if need be, in menial ways.

In verse 14, we see how Jesus gave His disciples that example by washing their feet and then telling them, *If I then, your Lord and Teacher (Master), have washed your feet, you ought [it is your duty, you are under obligation, you owe it] to wash one another's feet.*

Jesus was not really talking only about literal foot washing. He was actually saying to the disciples and to us, "Help each other. Take care of each other. Do for one another. Meet each other's needs."

Remember, Jesus said in verse 17, *If you know these things, blessed and happy and to be envied are you if you practice them [if you act accordingly and really do them].*

You and I are not going to be blessed because we know we should do good things for other people. We are not going to be blessed because we know we should have a servant's attitude. We are going to be blessed because we do what Jesus did.

Reaching the goal of serving others means living the way Jesus would live — and with God's help, we can reach that goal. But it takes time and effort.

The more we adapt ourselves to the ways of Jesus, the more His blessings will fill our lives.

Ways to Serve

For I have given you this as an example, so that you should do [in your turn] what I have done to you.

I assure you, most solemnly I tell you, A servant is not greater than his master, and no one who is sent is superior to the one who sent him.

JOHN 13:15,16

We all serve in different ways. I serve people by bringing them the Word of God and by preparing and studying and living my life in such a way that they can respect me. My daughter Sandra serves in another way. For example, if I needed a drink of water while I was preaching, she would be the one to jump up and go get it. She has the ministry of being a helper.

Now many times people are willing to do in church for some preacher or someone else they admire what they won't do at home.

I know that in any of my meetings I could say, "Oh, my water glass is empty; sister or brother in the third row, would you run and get me some water?" and that person would just think that was grand: "Oh, Joyce asked *me* to get her water!"

But then that same person could go home, and their spouse could say, "Honey, would you get me a glass of water?" and they might respond, "Get your own water. Do you think I am a slave around here?"

That is not the attitude God wants us to have.

A Servant's Attitude

. . . Jesus, knowing (fully aware) that the Father had put everything into His hands, and that He had come from God and was [now] returning to God,

Got up from supper, took off His garments, and taking a [servant's] towel, He fastened it around His waist.

Then He poured water into the washbasin and began to wash the disciples' feet and to wipe them with the [servant's] towel with which He was girded.

JOHN 13:3-5

Imagine — Jesus Christ, the Son of God, the Lord of glory, took off His garment, put on a servant's towel, knelt down and washed feet. Do you know why He did that? Because nobody else was moving to do it.

Earlier, the disciples had been having an argument about which one of them was the greatest.[3] Someone had to wash their feet before they could eat; it was a Jewish custom. So Jesus, as an example, knowing what was in their hearts, knowing Who He was and where He came from, took it upon Himself to be a servant to them all.

You and I cannot be a servant if we don't know who we are in Christ.[4] We will always be trying to prove something. We won't be able to do anything like Jesus did for the disciples because we will always have to do something big; otherwise, we won't think we are important.

Jesus got up, put on a servant's towel and washed the disciples' feet. He did that as an example, showing them how to live — by serving others.[5] Then He explained to them, "If you *do* what you have seen Me do, you will be blessed."[6]

We need to be doers of the Word and not just hearers.

You and I have all kinds of opportunities to be doers of the Word that we let pass us by all the time.

A friend may say to us, "Could you give me a ride into town?"

But we respond, "That's twenty minutes out of my way, and I've really got to get on home."

In situations like that we ought to realize that it is good for us to go out of our way now and then. Sometimes it is good for us to stretch ourselves a little bit to help somebody else.

Someone may say to us, "I've got to move this weekend, and I don't have a truck. Could you bring your truck over Saturday morning and help me for a couple of hours?"

"Well, ordinarily I would," we say, "but I didn't plan to do that on Saturday, and I've got some things I need to do."

Now obviously there are times when we have to say no because we do need time for ourselves. We can't spend all our time doing things for other people. But we certainly need to have a balance in doing our part. As a person "in Christ," our actions should demonstrate love, not selfishness and self-centeredness.

I have discovered by experience that my joy increases as my selfishness decreases.

Build Your House on the Rock

So everyone who hears these words of Mine and acts upon them [obeying them] will be like a sensible (prudent, practical, wise) man who built his house upon the rock.

And the rain fell and the floods came and the winds beat against that house; yet it did not fall, because it had been founded on the rock.

MATTHEW 7:24,25

Our house is not built upon a rock because we *hear* the Word. Our house is built upon a rock because we *do* the Word.

And everyone who hears these words of Mine and does not do them will be like a stupid (foolish) man who built his house upon the sand.

And the rain fell and the floods came and the winds blew and beat against that house, and it fell — and great and complete was the fall of it.

MATTHEW 7:26,27

Do you know what we do sometimes? When we get into a big mess, then we start doing what's right. As soon as we get relief, we go back to the way we were. Then we get into another big mess so we start making promises to God.

"Oh, Lord, I promise I'm going to pray more, I'm going to study the Word more, I'm going to give more, I'm going to treat people nicer."

God delivers us out of the mess, and pretty soon we drift back into doing things the way we used to.

The Israelites followed that same pattern over and over again. They turned to the Lord and were obedient to Him when things looked bad, but as soon as things got better, they went back to their old ways and forgot about Him and His Word. Then, when things they were doing didn't work the way they expected, they wondered (as we sometimes do), *What's wrong?*

What Works and What Doesn't Work

Then all those virgins got up and put their lamps in order.

And the foolish said to the wise, Give us some of your oil, for our lamps are going out.

But the wise replied, There will not be enough for us and for you; go instead to the dealers and buy for yourselves.

MATTHEW 25:7-9

Look at the life of a truly committed, dedicated Christian, and then look at the life of an excuse waiting to happen — someone who is a murmurer, a grumbler, a complainer, someone who feels sorry for themselves. Compare the fruit in their lives, and it won't take very long to figure out what works and what doesn't work.

It is like the difference between the five foolish virgins and the five wise virgins. The five foolish virgins didn't want to take any extra oil for their lamps. When the time came to welcome the bridegroom, their lamps had run out of oil. So they wanted to borrow some from the wise virgins, who had gone the extra mile and made sure to bring a full supply of oil.

People who never want to do anything extra get on my nerves. Sometimes they get on my last nerve because when the chips are down, they want my extra oil that I worked hard for, that I obeyed God to get.

There is a time to do for people what they ask of us, and there is also a time to say, "Sorry, you'll have to get your own oil."

We don't always help people by doing everything for them. That type of behavior can actually contribute to their problems because it helps them never take responsibility on their own. It is very difficult when you really love someone to not meet all their needs, but if they are not doing their part, it really does help them in the long run.

Do the Word

But be doers of the Word [obey the message], and not merely listeners to it, betraying yourselves [into deception by reasoning contrary to the Truth].

For if anyone only listens to the Word without obeying it and being a doer of it, he is like a man who looks carefully at his [own] natural face in a mirror;

For he thoughtfully observes himself, and then goes off and promptly forgets what he was like.

JAMES 1:22-24

You and I can look at ourselves in the mirror, and then five minutes later not remember what we are wearing unless we look again.

Well, the Word of God is like a mirror. We look in it, and we see what we are supposed to do. But it doesn't matter how many Christian teaching tapes we listen to or how many Christian conferences we attend or how many notes we take at those conferences; if we go away and forget what we have heard and seen, what good does it really do us?

Oh, we may be proud of ourselves because we have head knowledge. We may have heard some of the Scriptures so often we can even quote them by heart. But what are we doing?

How do we treat other people? Are we doing anything to make someone else's life better? What is our prayer life like? How much peace do we walk in? Are we *doers* of the Word or only *hearers?*

With knowledge comes responsibility.

The Responsibility of Knowing

So any person who knows what is right to do but does not do it, to him it is sin.

JAMES 4:17

Do you realize that every time we read the Bible, we take on more responsibility? Every time we attend a Bible teaching conference, we take on more responsibility. Every time we turn on a Christian television or radio program, we take on more responsibility. Why? Because we are getting educated, and we become responsible before God for what we know.

With the knowledge that we have been given power and authority to tread on the enemy and all his demons,[7] that we are to resist the devil and he will flee from us,[8] we become responsible before God to overcome adversity.

But how do we do that?

In Part 2 of this book, you will discover that Satan may have a plan for our destruction, but God already has a plan for our deliverance and victory.

If you will be diligent, with God's help, to do the things in Part 2 of this book, you will find yourself enjoying new and higher levels of victory rather than always being the victim.

Part 2:

Eight Ways to Overcome Adversity

Introduction

Finally, my brethren, be strong in the Lord and in the power of His might.

Put on the whole armor of God, that you may be able to stand against the wiles of the devil.

For we do not wrestle against flesh and blood, but against principalities, against powers, against the rulers of the darkness of this age, against spiritual hosts of wickedness in the heavenly places.

Therefore take up the whole armor of God, that you may be able to withstand in the evil day, and having done all, to stand.

EPHESIANS 6:10-13 NKJV

In the second part of this book, I would like to share with you several ways to overcome adversity. I believe that there is no hope of defeating Satan without a revelation concerning this subject.

You may be experiencing an attack against your mind, against your health, against your finances, against your family, against some other area of your life. How can you fight the devil, who is the source of these attacks? How can you overcome his schemes, enforce his defeat and keep him under your feet?

Praise is one way. Other ways include speaking the Word of God back to Satan when he says something to you in your thoughts and walking in love instead of leading a selfish lifestyle.

We will be looking at eight ways in all. While there may be more than eight ways, however many there are, they are not works of the flesh. They are things that we need to do, with God's help, to defeat the enemy and win the battle against him in the spiritual realm.

Remember, before you can become responsible for overcoming adversity, you must know the truth of how to do that. The truth will set you free[1] and keep the devil under your feet where he belongs.

That is why Satan does not want you to know these truths. His secret weapon, deception, is the primary weapon that he uses to furiously fight the good plan of God in your life. But Satan doesn't have a chance against you with these truths in your heart and God on your side.

4

REMAIN PEACEFUL IN THE STORM

Way #1

Stand therefore, having girded your waist with truth, having put on the breastplate of righteousness,

and having shod your feet with the preparation of the gospel of peace.

EPHESIANS 6:14,15 NKJV

As we have already seen, Ephesians chapter 6 says that we do not war against flesh and blood but against principalities and powers and wickedness in high places. It talks about the various pieces of armor that we are to put on and wear in order to stand against the enemy, who is out to destroy us.

Let's take a closer look at one of those pieces of armor — shoes of peace.

Now feet have to do with walking. We put on shoes so our feet won't get cut, banged up and bloody.

There is an analogy in that passage. The apostle Paul is trying to tell us, "If you want to make it through this life without having the devil beat your head off, then you have got to walk in peace."

"I wish I had some peace," you may say.

If you want peace in your life, then you have got to be a peacemaker and a peace maintainer. You can't just wait for peace to fall upon you. You've got to go after it.

Pursue Peace

Depart from evil and do good; seek, inquire for, and crave peace and pursue (go after) it!

PSALM 34:14

This Psalm instructs us to pursue peace, to inquire for, crave and go after it. If you want peace bad enough, you will make whatever changes you need to make in your life to see that you get it.

Maybe you are frustrated and stressed out all the time. If so, you may need to cut a few things out of your life.

"But I want to do all those things."

Then the result will be frustration and stress. You are the one who makes your schedule. You are the only one who can change it.

If you want peace in your life, *don't exceed your limits.*

Nobody says you have to do all the things you are doing. Start looking at your life, figure out which things in it are not bearing any fruit and start pruning them, just as you would prune dead branches off a tree.

It is so important to not overcommit yourself.

"But my kids have got to go to baseball practice on Monday night and hockey practice on Tuesday night and band practice on Wednesday night."

No, your kids don't have to do everything they want to do. They need to do something; it's good for them to be involved in some activities. But you can't let their schedule control your whole family.

I didn't do anything outside of school when I was growing up, and I survived. I was given just so many minutes to get home after school, and that was it. I took part in almost no school activities and had very little contact with anyone outside of school. Yet today God is using me to touch the lives of millions of people around the world through this ministry.

My daughter Sandra was on a swim team that met right in our neighborhood so I didn't have to take her; she walked there. She was also on a soft-ball team for a while. That was the extent of her school involvement, besides attending classes every day, and she survived. In fact, today she is a part of this ministry and speaks to several hundred thousand people every year.

Once again I am not saying that you have to be just like us. But I want you to get a hold of the fact that trying to make sure your kids are the most popular ones in school can be bad for both you and them. Sometimes all it does is get them in trouble.

Let your kids do some things. But know that it is all right if you have to say to them, "You can do this, but not that." They may not like it, but they will get over it. Those who get sad get glad again.

We need to follow God's leading as to what we — and our children — are to be involved in and where we are to use our energy. We must learn to say yes when God says yes and no when He says no. When we are obedient to His leading, we will be able to accomplish what He gives us to do and enjoy a peaceful life.

Adjust to Others

Live in harmony with one another; do not be haughty (snobbish, high-minded, exclusive), but readily adjust yourself to [people, things] and give yourselves to humble tasks. Never overestimate yourself or be wise in your own conceits.

Repay no one evil for evil, but take thought for what is honest and proper and noble [aiming to be above reproach] in the sight of everyone.

If possible, as far as it depends on you, live at peace with everyone.

ROMANS 12:16-18

Do whatever you have to do to get peace in your life. If that means you have to shut up once in a while and not keep arguing with somebody about something, then do it. Sometimes it is better to just walk away and let everyone calm down.

The Bible doesn't say that everybody is going to adapt to you; it says that you should adjust yourself to them.

We are told in Romans 16:20 that the God of all peace will soon crush Satan under our feet. I don't believe that you are ever going to keep Satan under your feet if you don't learn to walk in peace.

Remain Constant and at Peace

And do not [for a moment] be frightened or intimidated in anything by your opponents and adversaries, for such [constancy and fearlessness] will be a clear sign (proof and seal) to them of [their impending] destruction, but [a sure token

*and evidence] of your deliverance and salvation,
and that from God.*

PHILIPPIANS 1:28

This Scripture tells you what to do when you are
being aggravated by the devil. You are to remain constant and fearless. The thing you don't want to do is
to become mad and upset. Satan is an expert at steal-
ing our joy, and getting mad and upset is precisely
what he wants you to do so you will become weak
and wimpy and give him a chance to overpower you.

When the enemy starts picking on you, you can
take your attention off what God wants you to do
and concentrate on the problem the devil has insti-
gated, or you can remain constant and at peace,
trusting God that He will take care of the situation.

Let God Handle It

*Now when they had left the multitude, they took
Him along in the boat as He was. And other little
boats were also with Him.*

*And a great windstorm arose, and the waves beat
into the boat, so that it was already filling.*

But He was in the stern, asleep on a pillow. And they awoke Him and said to Him, "Teacher, do You not care that we are perishing?"

Then He arose and rebuked the wind, and said to the sea, "Peace, be still!" And the wind ceased and there was a great calm.

But He said to them, "Why are you so fearful? How is it that you have no faith?"

MARK 4:36-40 NKJV

In this passage, Jesus rebuked the disciples because they did not hold their peace in the storm.

They were worried and upset, but Jesus was sleeping peacefully in the back of the boat. They came to Him, woke Him up and cried out, "Jesus! There's a terrible storm going on! What are You going to do?"

Jesus woke up and quickly handled the situation. Then He turned to the terrified disciples and said to them, "Why are you so fearful?" In other words, "There's nothing to fear; I AM[1] is with you."

Jesus is always with us in every situation that is at hand. *The believer who is experiencing God's peace through His Son Jesus can have peace even in the middle of the storms of life.*

At those times, you don't have to know what the Lord is going to do or when He is going to do it. You just need to know that if He is there with you in the storm — which He is — then He will take care of the situation.

The bottom line is, you will never have the edge over the devil if you don't learn to hold your peace.

Hold Your Peace and Remain at Rest

The Lord made hard and strong the heart of Pharaoh king of Egypt, and he pursued the Israelites, for [they] left proudly and defiantly.

The Egyptians pursued them, all the horses and chariots of Pharaoh and his horsemen and his army, and overtook them encamped at the [Red] Sea. . . .

When Pharaoh drew near, the Israelites looked up, and behold, the Egyptians were marching after them; and the Israelites were exceedingly frightened and cried out to the Lord.

And they said to Moses, Is it because there are no graves in Egypt that you have taken us away to die in the wilderness? Why have you treated us this way and brought us out of Egypt?

EXODUS 14:8-11

At God's command, Moses led the Israelites out of bondage in Egypt. Then, when the Egyptians pursued them, all of a sudden it became Moses' fault that the enemy was after them.

Isn't that the way we are? We go through a difficult situation, and we begin to complain and try to find someone to blame for our predicament the same way the Israelites did with Moses.

Did we not tell you in Egypt, Let us alone; let us serve the Egyptians? For it would have been better for us to serve the Egyptians than to die in the wilderness.

Moses told the people, Fear not; stand still (firm, confident, undismayed) and see the salvation of the Lord which He will work for you today. For the Egyptians you have seen today you shall never see again.

The Lord will fight for you, and you shall hold your peace and remain at rest.

EXODUS 14:12-14

Sometimes it seems as though God does not fight for us, as though He does not come against the enemy and defeat him for us. The reason this happens is that we are not holding our peace and remaining at rest. God wants to help us, but He wants to do it His way and not our way — because our way usually involves being upset, which causes worry, fretfulness, reasoning and anxiety.

When the enemy is coming against you, the most powerful thing you can do is refuse to let it upset you.

One time during a series of meetings I was holding, my daughter Sandra came and told me that some man was outside the building telling people not to come in. He was handing out tracts and telling people, "Don't go listen to her; she shouldn't be doing what she's doing."

When Sandra told me what was happening, at first I was concerned and felt like doing something about it.

Then I thought, *No, I'm not going to get involved with that.*

My head was saying, *What if people get scared and won't come in?*

But no one who knows me and has watched me on television is going to let one person standing outside the building and making negative remarks about me keep them from coming in to listen to me.

We went ahead with our meeting, and the session was full. The power of God could be felt so strongly in the service; God ministered to the people by working through me to meet their needs.[2] Deciding to trust God and not lose my peace over that situation resulted in many people being blessed by Him during that time.

Sitting Is Resting

But God, being rich in mercy, because of His great love with which He loved us, even when we were dead in our transgressions, made us alive together with Christ (by grace you have been saved),

and raised us up with Him, and seated us with Him in the heavenly places, in Christ Jesus.

EPHESIANS 2:4-6 NASB

This passage says that we are seated in heavenly places with Christ Jesus.

I read past that passage one day, and the Holy Spirit stopped me. I just felt that I had missed something so I went back and read it again: *God . . . seated us with Him in the heavenly places, in Christ Jesus.* I still didn't get it. So I went back and read it once more: *God . . . seated us with Him. . . .* Finally I got it: We are seated; we are *seated.*

Then I started thinking of how Jesus is depicted in the Bible after His resurrection and ascension. As in this passage, He is often depicted as being seated at the right hand of the Father.[3]

Do you know what people do when they sit? They rest.

To be seated in heavenly places with Jesus is to enter an "inner rest."

Jesus is resting; according to the Bible, He is waiting for His enemies to be made a footstool for His feet.[4]

We rest while we wait on God. Isaiah 40:31 teaches us that waiting on God is expecting, looking for and hoping in Him. It's spending time with Him in His Word and in His Presence. We don't worry while we wait on God. We don't get frustrated while we wait on God. We don't get upset while we wait on God. We rest.

Sometimes when you start to get nervous and upset, anxious or worried, you just need to tell yourself, "Sit down." That does not mean just your physical body; it also means your soul — your mind, will and emotions. It is important to let our entire being rest.

Under the Old Covenant, when the high priest went into the Holy of Holies to make blood sacrifices for the sins of the people, he did not sit down.

It seems very unlikely that there was a chair in there because the Bible doesn't mention it.[5] The requirements were so stringent that he did what he had to do and left. He could not rest in the Presence of God.

I have been told that the high priest wore bells on his robe[6] and that he had a rope tied to his waist. If the bells quit ringing, the people outside the Holy of Holies knew that he had done something wrong and had died, so they pulled him out.

There is such a lesson in that. It symbolizes how people could not rest in God's Presence under the Old Covenant. The Old Covenant had many laws and was based upon works. But, thank God, the New Covenant is based upon the work Jesus has accomplished, not on our own merits or works.

Jesus, our High Priest, Who went into the Holy of Holies with His own blood, put it on the mercy seat in heaven and sat down. Now the atonement for the sins of the world is finished.[7]

If you have read the last book of the Bible, you
know who wins the war. So if you are struggling,
take a seat and rest. The promise of God's peace is
not made to those who work and struggle in their
own strength but to those who sit and rest in
Christ Jesus — and stay in their spiritual seat
instead of jumping up every few minutes and
getting out of rest.

God Works While You Rest

*For he who has once entered [God's] rest also has
ceased from [the weariness and pain] of human
labors, just as God rested from those labors pecu-
liarly His own.*

*Let us therefore be zealous and exert ourselves and
strive diligently to enter that rest. . . .*

HEBREWS 4:10,11

Notice verse 11 again: *Let us therefore be zealous
and exert ourselves and strive diligently. . . .* In other
words, our job is not to change our husbands, our
wives, our kids; it's not to change our circumstances or build our ministries. Our job is to enter

the rest of God and to believe that while we are resting, God is working.

Peace Is Our Inheritance

Peace I leave with you; My [own] peace I now give and bequeath to you. Not as the world gives do I give to you. Do not let your hearts be troubled, neither let them be afraid. [Stop allowing yourselves to be agitated and disturbed; and do not permit yourselves to be fearful and intimidated and cowardly and unsettled.]

JOHN 14:27

Whenever I face something that is disturbing, frightful or unsettling, I hold my peace, and God takes care of the situation. It took me years and years to learn how to do that.

It was part of my heritage in the Promised Land of God's promises to have the kind of peace I have now. But I never possessed it because I didn't dispossess the devil by refusing to let him upset me.

The devil sets us up to get us upset. That's why Jesus left us His peace as our inheritance and told us, "Stop allowing yourselves to be upset and disturbed."

We have something to do with whether the devil is able to upset us. If you know anything about Satan, he doesn't have any power. First Peter 5:8 KJV says, . . . *the devil, as a roaring lion, walketh about, seeking whom he may devour.* Notice that verse says *may* and not *will.* The only power Satan has is the power we give him.

Getting us upset is one of the devil's favorite tactics. If he can control us by getting us upset with circumstances, then he will have us under his thumb all the time. But we don't have to give in to him. Peace in the midst of tribulation is our inheritance, but many Christians never use this great benefit even though it belongs to us.

Remember this: When you are attacked, stay in peace. That tells the devil he is defeated. He doesn't know what to do with you if he cannot get you upset.

5

SPEND TIME WITH GOD

Way #2

. . . let everyone who is godly pray — pray to You in a time when You may be found; surely when the great waters [of trial] overflow, they shall not reach [the spirit in] him.

PSALM 32:6

The first thing you need to do to overcome adversity is to remain peaceful in the storm. The second thing is to spend time with God.

"But, Joyce, I just don't have time."

You have the same amount of time as anybody else. We all get an equal allotment of time — twenty-four hours a day, no more and no less — and we all spend it on something. You can spend it in front of the television. You can spend it arguing. You can spend it shopping. You can spend it combing your hair and putting on makeup. You can spend it cutting the grass. Or you can spend it with God.

"I don't have time" is an excuse. I know because I used it for a long time about exercise. My husband, Dave, agrees with that statement because he has exercised every other day most of his life.

Dave makes time for exercise because it's important to him. For years I always said, "I don't have time," when the truth was, I didn't like it, and I didn't want to do it.

People who want something bad enough pay the price to get it.

Let's be honest. What we really want to do, we make time for. Some of us watch television more hours a week than we spend with God. As I said, we find time to do what we want to do.

It's simple: You are not going to overcome the adversities Satan sends your way if you don't spend time with God. Why? Because you are protected by the Presence of God.

Protected in His Presence

Oh, how great is Your goodness, which You have laid up for those who fear, revere, and worship You, goodness which You have wrought for those who trust and take refuge in You before the sons of men!

In the secret place of Your presence You hide them from the plots of men; You keep them secretly in Your pavilion from the strife of tongues.

Psalm 31:19,20

The secret place mentioned in verse 20 is the place of God's Presence. When we spend time with the Lord in prayer and in His Word, we are in the secret place. This secret place is a place of peace and security, a place where we can give Him our cares and trust Him to take care of us.

One of the ways that the enemy attacks us is through other people coming against us, talking about us, judging us or criticizing us. Verse 20 of this passage tells us God hides us from the plots of men and keeps us from the strife of tongues.

When we spend time in God's Presence, He becomes our protection, our stability, our place of refuge. He becomes the Source of our help, not only when others want to hurt us and speak evil against us but in every situation and circumstance.

How do I know that what people say about me can't hurt me? It is because I spend time with God.

In Isaiah 54:17 we are told: *But no weapon that is formed against you shall prosper, and every tongue that shall rise against you in judgment you shall show to be in the wrong. This [peace, righteousness, security, triumph over opposition] is the heritage of the servants of the Lord. . . .*

This is part of your heritage as a believer: If you spend time with God, you are protected by His Presence. No matter what anybody says about you, it is not really going to make any difference because sooner or later they will be shown to be in the wrong.

"Don't Send Me without Your Presence!"

Moses said to the Lord, See, You say to me, Bring up this people, but You have not let me know whom You will send with me. . . .

And the Lord said, My Presence shall go with you, and I will give you rest.

And Moses said to the Lord, If Your Presence does not go with me, do not carry us up from here!

EXODUS 33:12,14,15

Moses was being called by God to go to Pharaoh and tell him, "Let my people go," and he was very concerned. He asked the Lord, "Who am I going to say sent me? Pharaoh is not going to listen to me and set the children of Israel free from Egyptian bondage."

Moses was scared; he was upset. But God said to him, "My Presence will go with you, and I'll give you rest."

I love Moses' reply: "Okay, but if Your Presence is not going to go with us, then don't send me!"

That's the way I feel when I start to go into one of my meetings to minister to others. "God, if You're not going to be there, don't send me!"

We need to really understand the awesomeness of the Presence of God and what is available to us as believers. Why in the world would we not want to spend time with God? We hang on the telephone, we hang out in the shopping center, we hang in front of the TV, and there is no problem. *But the devil fights us more on spending time with God than he does on any other part of our Christian life.*

In fact, Satan would like nothing better than for us to get involved in all kinds of religious activity rather than spend time with the Lord.

There is only one way I know to maintain the anointing on my life and that is by spending time in the Presence of God.

You may be wondering, *But what do I do when I spend time with God?*

You just dedicate a portion of time for that purpose. Try not to be legalistic about it, but do try to be as regular with it as you can. During that time period, read the Bible and any other Christian books that minister to you. Talk to God. Sometimes you may want to listen to Christian music and worship; other times you may just want to sit there and enjoy the silence. If you will do that, you will begin to feel and sense the Presence of the Lord.

One of the things we need more than anything is a conscious awareness of God's Presence with us.

Can You Hear the Birds?

For thus said the Lord God, the Holy One of Israel: In returning [to Me] and resting [in Me] you shall be saved; in quietness and in [trusting] confidence shall be your strength. . . .

ISAIAH 30:15

Our lives are so busy and so noisy. We don't have enough solitude; we don't spend enough time being alone. We don't have enough silence; we don't spend enough time sitting somewhere with no noise.

For example, we always think we've got to have something on in our home — the radio, the television, the stereo, the computer — but that is not true. One of the best ways to experience the Presence of God is to get it quiet enough in your house to hear the birds outside.

Get Refilled

And after He had dismissed the multitudes, He went up into the hills by Himself to pray. When it was evening, He was still there alone.

MATTHEW 14:23

If you want to have victory in your daily life, spend time alone with God.

Jesus took regular times away for prayer and fellowship. He apparently had a sense that any time He felt He had given out all that He had in Him, He would walk away from everybody and go somewhere, get by Himself, pray, talk to God — just do whatever He did in those times of solitude. Then He would come back ready to minister again.

Don't let yourself get burned out. When you feel you have given out all you have in you, then go spend some time with God and get refilled. When your gas tank is getting low, you go and get it filled up again so you won't run out of gas. But when it comes to spiritual things, you may be running on fumes.

At times Jesus went off into the mountains to pray. He'd get up early in the morning to be alone with God. When He had a serious decision to make, sometimes He prayed all night. Why? He knew the value of being in the Presence of God.

Run to the Throne

Come to Me, all you who labor and are heavy-laden and overburdened, and I will cause you to rest. [I will ease and relieve and refresh your souls.]

Take My yoke upon you and learn of Me, for I am gentle (meek) and humble (lowly) in heart, and you will find rest (relief and ease and refreshment and recreation and blessed quiet) for your souls.

MATTHEW 11:28,29

When you are upset, go to Jesus and spend a little time with Him. When you hear something that bothers you or hurts you, when you learn that someone has been talking about you behind your back, take it to Jesus. When you hear there is going to be a layoff at work, run to the Lord.

If I heard something like that, I would go immediately to the Lord and say, "Well, Jesus, I guess You have heard that people are saying there's going to be a layoff at work. I am putting my order in early just in case: If I do get laid off, I am asking You for a job that is even better than the one I have right now."

Don't run to the phone; run to the throne.

Honor God by Putting Him First

But seek (aim at and strive after) first of all His kingdom and His righteousness (His way of doing and being right), and then all these things taken together will be given you besides.

MATTHEW 6:33

We need to honor God by putting Him first. We need to run to Him first, listen to Him first, give Him the first part of our money, the first part of our time, the first part of everything in our life. According to this Scripture, when we do that, He will supply our needs and bless us.

Do you know what Dave and I usually do the first thing in the morning? We get up, have some coffee, sit and talk for a few minutes and maybe have a bite to eat. Then each of us goes to our own separate area, and we probably spend a couple of hours with the Lord.

I remember years ago when I would finish a series of meetings, the next day I would think, *Well, I worked all weekend. I want to do something else today.*

I soon learned that I can't survive if I don't get some spiritual rest and renewal, especially after holding a meeting. I came to realize that without it, I'll be tired the next day. I need to be built back up. I need to be refilled. After I have spent time feeding others, then I need to be fed.

Who feeds me?

Jesus!

And He wants to do the same for all His children.

Joy Is Strength

You will show me the path of life; in Your presence is fullness of joy, at Your right hand there are pleasures forevermore.

Psalm 16:11

The psalmist says that in the Presence of the Lord there is fullness of joy.

When you have joy, you have strength. According to Nehemiah 8:10, . . . *the joy of the Lord is your strength* . . . not your circumstances. If you have His strength, you can overcome the devil's schemes all the time.

You will have little or no strength against the devil if you allow your circumstances to determine your joy. So when you feel depressed, when you feel sad, when you feel like you don't know where your joy has gone, get in the Presence of God.

Sometimes when I spend time with God, I will start out crying because I am bothered about something, and end up laughing.

Have you ever spent time with God all by yourself and ended up laughing like a silly person, just laughing and laughing? Do you ever feel kind of silly just sitting in a room by yourself laughing?

My husband sometimes walks into my room when I am by myself, laughing. He just looks at me and says, "Okay, I'll see you later." In our house we know what that is — the joy of the Lord that comes from dwelling in the secret place of His Presence.

Dwell in the Secret Place

He who dwells in the secret place of the Most High shall remain stable and fixed under the shadow of the Almighty [Whose power no foe can withstand].
Psalm 91:1

The secret place is a hiding place, a place of protection, a place with a covering over it so we will be kept safe from all our enemies. If we spend time in the Presence of God, dwelling in that secret place, the devil can't defeat us.

Let's look for a moment at some instances in the Bible where the Presence of God is mentioned.

Psalm 53:2 says that God looks to see who seeks, or desperately requires, His Presence. The Old

Testament describes how the Israelites always sent the Ark of the Covenant into battle first because the Ark carried the Presence of God.[1]

One instance in the New Testament describes how the disciples had spent much time with Jesus before His death, burial and resurrection. After His ascension into heaven,[2] two of the disciples, Peter and John, were ministering to some people. The religious leaders were outraged at their message about Jesus so they arrested them and began to question them about what they were doing.

According to Acts 4:13, when those leaders saw the disciples' boldness and eloquence of speech and *. . . perceived that they were unlearned and untrained in the schools [common men with no educational advantages], they marveled; and they recognized that they had been with Jesus.*

When you have been with Jesus, there is just something about you that is different from the average, ordinary person. Spending time in the secret place of His Presence changes you from what you are to what only He can make you to be.

6

WATCH YOUR MOUTH

Way #3

Death and life are in the power of the tongue, and they who indulge in it shall eat the fruit of it [for death or life].

PROVERBS 18:21

The third way of defeating Satan is with words.

Words are so awesome. Words are containers for power. They carry either creative power or destructive power. For example, in my conferences I speak words, and those who hear those words receive life — life in their relationships, in their ministries and in all kinds of areas that God uses me to speak to them about.

Jesus said that His words are spirit, and they are life.[1] But people can also speak death to you by speaking things that put a heaviness on you.

Proverbs 18:21 is a Scripture that I am very familiar with, but I always get blessed by it every time I read it. As we saw, it talks about death and life being in the power of the tongue and how those who indulge in it will eat its fruit, either for death or for life.

In this verse the writer is saying, "Every time you open your mouth, you are ministering death or life, and whatever you dish out is what you are going to eat."

We have heard the phrase "You're going to have to eat your words," and it is so true.

You may be eating your words right now, and that's why you don't like your life — because of your mouth.

I have written a book called *"Me and My Big Mouth!"* that deals with the words we speak and how to make them work for us instead of against us. The subtitle of the book is *Your Answer Is Right Under Your Nose.*

You may be reading this book about overcoming adversity because you are desperately looking for an answer to what is happening in your life. Do you believe that it is even remotely possible that your answer could be in changing the way you talk?

Be More Thankful

Make a joyful noise to the Lord, all you lands!

Serve the Lord with gladness! Come before His presence with singing!

Know (perceive, recognize, and understand with approval) that the Lord is God! It is He Who has made us, not we ourselves [and we are His]! We are His people and the sheep of His pasture.

Enter into His gates with thanksgiving and a thank offering and into His courts with praise! Be thankful and say so to Him, bless and affectionately praise His name!

PSALM 100:1-4

One example of changing the way you talk may
be in giving thanks to God. We all need to be more
thankful. We all need to do a lot less complaining
and a lot more thanking.

Psalm 100:4 says, . . . *Be thankful and say so*. . . .
If you are thankful, say so. If there are people in
your life you appreciate, say so. If you appreciate
your family and friends, if you appreciate your
pastor, say so. If you appreciate everything that
God is doing in your life, say so.

We need to open our mouth and give thanks.
We don't have any trouble getting our mouth open
when we don't like something. We need to learn to
use our mouth for the purpose God gave it to us.
He didn't give it to us to hurt people by engaging in
negative, gossipy, judgmental, critical, backbiting
talk. He gave it to us to love people through our
encouraging, positive, life-giving words.

Remember, words are powerful.

Speak a Word in Due Season

*[The Servant of God says] The Lord God has given
Me the tongue of a disciple and of one who is*

taught, that I should know how to speak a word in season to him who is weary. . . .

ISAIAH 50:4

This Scripture says that we as disciples should learn how to speak a word to the weary in due season. Think about that. A word (just one word) to a weary person (someone who is ready to quit, ready to give up) spoken in due season (right when they need it) can change a person. It can turn their whole life around, keep them from backsliding or from giving up, and urge them forward.

We all have a ministry. That ministry is to give the weary a word — a word in due season — and bless them with the words of our mouth.

Speaking words in due season to one another will keep us from growing weary.

The Word Is a Weapon

Above all, taking the shield of faith with which you will be able to quench all the fiery darts of the wicked one.

And take the helmet of salvation, and the sword of the Spirit, which is the word of God.

EPHESIANS 6:16,17 NKJV

Earlier in this book we talked about the armor of God, which believers are to put on in order to wage spiritual warfare and overcome adversity. One important part of that armor is the sword of the Spirit, which is the Word of God.

We need to know the Word of God because it is powerful. We need to study it and learn it, then speak it out according to our situations and our needs.

The Word of God is a weapon for us to use when the enemy comes against us. The devil is afraid of the Word because he knows there is power in it.

The Word of God coming out of the believer's mouth is a sharp sword against the enemy.

When you feel yourself getting depressed, don't say, "I'm depressed." Take hold of the Word and say, "The Lord has given me the garment of praise for the spirit of heaviness."[2] Say, "Why are you so downcast, O my soul? Put your hope in God."[3] You will be absolutely amazed and awestruck at how your life will change if you change the way you talk.

We are told in the Bible that we serve a God Who calls things that be not as though they were,[4] a God Who speaks of nonexistent things as if they already existed.[5] You and I need to do the same thing. If we know something is in the Word, we need to speak it forth.

Satan is a liar. He is described in the Bible as . . . *the father of lies and of all that is false.*[6] He strives to give us trouble and then uses it to influence us to prophesy that same kind of trouble in our future.

How are you talking about your life? How do you talk about your future? As you will see later on in this chapter, you can prophesy a better future for yourself and your loved ones according to God's Word by prophesying the Word over the dead areas of your lives.

Defeat Satan with the Word

And Jesus replied to him, [The Scripture] says, You shall not tempt (try, test exceedingly) the Lord your God.

And when the devil had ended every [the complete cycle of] temptation, he [temporarily] left Him [that is, stood off from Him] until another more opportune and favorable time.

LUKE 4:12,13

You can defeat Satan with the Word of God, just as Jesus did.

At the time of Jesus' baptism in the river Jordan, *the Holy Spirit descended upon Him in bodily form like a dove, and a voice came from heaven, saying, You are My Son, My Beloved! In You I am well pleased and find delight!*[7]

Afterwards, Jesus was led by the Holy Spirit out into the wilderness to be tempted by the devil for forty days and forty nights. Immediately Satan started coming against Him, tempting Him to do certain things to prove that He was the Son of God.

To each temptation offered by the devil, Jesus said, *It is written. . . .*

The Bible says that Satan said to Jesus, and Jesus said to Satan; the devil said to Jesus, and Jesus said to the devil.

People always tell me what the devil is saying to them, but I want to know what they are saying to the devil.

From this passage we get a revelation of the importance of learning how to talk back to the devil. We need to get that sword out of its sheath and begin to use it on the enemy.

When the devil tells you that you are no good, open your mouth and begin to say good things about yourself: "I am the righteousness of God in Jesus Christ.[8] I prosper in everything I lay my hands to. I have gifts and talents, and God is using me. I walk in love. Joy flows through me. I am an overcomer who is precious in God's sight, and He loves me."

In review, if you want to overcome adversity, stay in peace, spend time with God and wield the two-edged sword of His Word against the enemy. You can defeat Satan with the Word of God.

Remember, . . . *the weapons of our warfare are not carnal, but mighty through God to the pulling down of strong holds. . . .*[9] We are fighting a spiritual war, not a natural war, and our weapons are spiritual weapons. God's Word is one of the most powerful spiritual weapons He has given us. To use it, meditate on and speak the positive things it says about you.

I get so excited about the Word because I have studied it long enough and have had enough experience with it to know what I am telling you will work if you will apply it in your life. You can change your future by prophesying over your own life what the Word of God says about you.

Don't go around saying, "Nothing good ever happens to me." Instead, say, "God has a good plan for my life, and I am going to see it come to pass."

If the devil says you are going to die, say, "I am going to live and not die, and I am going to be here to recount and tell aloud the works of the Lord."[10]

When you learn the Scriptures, then you can speak the Scriptures. There really is life and power in the Word of God — but not in a negative confession.

Exercise Control

We should not tempt the Lord [try His patience, become a trial to Him, critically appraise Him, and exploit His goodness] as some of them did — and were killed by poisonous serpents;

Nor discontentedly complain as some of them did — and were put out of the way entirely by the destroyer (death).

1 CORINTHIANS 10:9,10

I got such a revelation for my own life out of this passage because, like the Israelites, I too was a grumbler, a murmurer and a faultfinder. Most people are the same way — even many Christians. There is not a man or a woman alive today who does not know how to murmur and complain.

As the above passage tells us, most of the Israelites died in the wilderness. As a matter of fact, all of the adults who came out of Egypt perished there, except two: Joshua and Caleb. Those Israelites who died in the wilderness had children, and some of those children went into the Promised Land.[11] But that is pretty amazing when you think about how many millions of people Moses led out of Egypt.

I have a powerful tape series called "Wilderness Mentalities." In it I talk about all the reasons that those people died out there in the wilderness and never made it through to the Promised Land. One reason was that they were murmurers and grumblers, complainers and faultfinders.

Every time something didn't go right, they found fault with Moses. Their negative attitude was just another part of their evil and carnal way of life, a way of life that included indulgence in immorality. In fact, as a result of that indulgence, one day twenty-three thousand of them fell dead.[12] And, remember, as a result of their complaining, they *were put out of the way entirely by the destroyer (death).*

Why did that happen? As 1 Corinthians 10:9 said, it happened because the people tempted the

Lord, tried His patience, became a trial to Him, criticized or critically appraised Him and exploited His goodness.

When we do not open our mouth and give thanks, but instead murmur and complain, we are exploiting the goodness of God because no matter what is going on in our life, God is still good.

When we read that those people died in the wilderness because of their negative, complaining lifestyle, I would think that if we had any sense at all, it would put the fear of God in us.

Now I'm not trying to say that if we murmur or complain about something, God is going to cause us to perish. But how many doors do we open for the devil in our lives through murmuring and complaining? How many times do we ask God to give us something, and after He gives it to us, we start murmuring and complaining because we have to take care of it?

We complain because we are not married and then complain because we are married. We complain because we don't have a big house; then we get a big house and complain because we have to clean it. This kind of wilderness mentality keeps us living in the wilderness when we could be living in the Promised Land — the land of abundance that Jesus died to give us.

In Philippians 2:14 the Bible tells us to do all things without complaining. "All things" means everything. We are to clean our house without complaining, mow our yard without complaining, drive to work without complaining, do our job without complaining.

We have got to get aggressive against the enemy in this area. Think about it. How much time do we spend complaining when having a good attitude would be at least 90 percent of the battle?

How easy it is for me to start complaining about everything I have to do in the ministry. Then all I have to do is remember all the years I prayed to have this ministry, and my attitude changes.

I am sure there are people on our travel team who pray, "Oh, God, give me something regular to do so I can stay home all the time." Then when they are doing something "regular," they complain, "I am so tired of this same old routine; I wish I could travel again." I am sure we have musicians who pray, "Oh, God, give me a job where I can travel and use my talent." Then they get that job, and they say, "I'm so tired. This hotel is so dumpy, and there is no good restaurant. I wish I could just stay home once in a while." The reason I know they must say those things is that I have said them myself many times.

We can accomplish anything and always be a winner as long as we have a godly attitude. We develop that kind of attitude by exercising control over our mouth daily. To eliminate anything that offends God in our conversation, our prayer should be continually, *Set a guard, O Lord, before my mouth; keep watch at the door of my lips.*[13]

Keep the Door Closed to Satan

He was oppressed, [yet when] He was afflicted, He was submissive and opened not His mouth; like a

lamb that is led to the slaughter, and as a sheep before
her shearers is dumb, so He opened not his mouth.
ISAIAH 53:7

Think about that Scripture. What do you think
it means by saying that Jesus didn't open His
mouth? It means that Jesus had enough sense to
know that when He was under pressure, He would
be tempted to say wrong things. So when He came
into the final days of His agony here on earth, He
said very little.

Jesus knew when it was about time for Him to
go to the cross. In John 14:30 He actually said to
His disciples, *I will not talk with you much more, for*
the prince (evil genius, ruler) of the world is coming.
And he has no claim on Me. [He has nothing in
common with Me; there is nothing in Me that
belongs to him, and he has no power over Me.]

Do you know what I believe He was saying?
"Satan is really coming on strong now, but he
hasn't got anything on Me, and I am not going to
open My mouth and say anything that might give
him an open door. So if I seem a little quiet now,

don't think too much about it. It's just that things are going to be getting tough for a while, and I don't want to talk out of My emotions."

I don't believe that any child of God wants to express the enemy's work, but many do by choosing to say what they think, feel and want instead of speaking God's Word. Choose to be God's mouthpiece, and close the door to the devil.

Words Carry Power

By faith we understand that the worlds [during the successive ages] were framed (fashioned, put in order, and equipped for their intended purpose) by the word of God, so that what we see was not made out of things which are visible.

HEBREWS 11:3

Words are not just empty vessels. They carry power. God created the earth with words. The Holy Spirit changes lives with words. People are encouraged or defeated because of words. Marriages break up because people don't say the right words.

How many marriages do you think would still be intact if one of the partners had just said every day of that marriage, "I love you, and I appreciate you"? It is just a few words, but those words carry power; they are positive, loving and encouraging.

Every time I finish preaching, I mean *every* time, no more than ten minutes go by before my husband says to me, "That was a really good message." And you know what? I need to hear that — especially from him.

I always try to tell those who lead the worship that they did a good job, and they need to hear that.

People don't need us to tear them down; they need us to build them up by speaking words to them that edify, exhort and encourage.

What Are You Saying?

The hand of the Lord was upon me, and He brought me out in the Spirit of the Lord and set me down in the midst of the valley; and it was full of bones.

And He caused me to pass round about among them, and behold, there were very many [human bones] in the open valley or plain, and behold, they were very dry.

And He said to me, Son of man, can these bones live? And I answered, O Lord God, You know!

Again He said to me, Prophesy to these bones and say to them, O you dry bones, hear the word of the Lord.

EZEKIEL 37:1-4

I am sure that at one time or another in your life you have felt that everywhere you looked there was a pile of dead, dry bones.

God showed those bones to Ezekiel and asked him, "Can these dead, dry bones live again?" In other words, He was asking, "Can anything be done with this mess? Can this situation change?"

Then He told Ezekiel to talk to the bones and say to them, "Oh, you dry bones, hear the Word of the Lord."

If you are in a big mess and you are trying to run the devil off of your property and out of your life, you can do it with words.

Can you get a hold of that? You can say, "Listen, you big mountain, hear the Word of the Lord. Listen, you big mess, hear the Word of the Lord. Listen, poverty, hear the Word of the Lord. Listen, sickness and disease, hear the Word of the Lord. Listen, you tormenting spirit, hear the Word of the Lord."

If you read the rest of that story in Ezekiel chapter 37, you will find that after Ezekiel had done as God told him to do and prophesied to those dry bones, they came together, sinews and flesh came upon them and skin covered them.

Then in verse 9 the Lord told Ezekiel to prophesy and command that breath and spirit come into them. In verse 10 Ezekiel said, *So I prophesied as He commanded me, and the breath and spirit came into [the bones], and they lived and stood up upon their feet, an exceedingly great host.*

All that happened because one man prophesied.

What are you saying to the dead, dry circumstances in your life? Are you prophesying to your dead bones? Or is what you are saying making them deader and dryer?

Maybe this sounds familiar to you: "Nothing in my life is ever going to change. Every time I get a dollar, the devil takes it away from me. It never fails; every time I think something good is going to happen, I get attacked."

If that is what you are saying, then you are just asking for more trouble. Every time you speak that way you're giving the devil the right to use his power.

Instead, learn how to speak to Satan and neutralize his power.

Don't tell the devil what you *feel* or what you *think* — don't look at your life and what you don't have — open your mouth and tell him exactly what God has promised you! Once you change your words, it's all over for him. There's really nothing he can do about it after that.

7

SUBMIT YOURSELF
TO GOD

Way #4

[Live] as children of obedience [to God]. . . .

1 PETER 1:14

When I talk about the necessity of obedience to God in overcoming adversity, I always clarify it by saying *personal* obedience. I do that because there are things that God will tell you to do or not to do that He may not be speaking to anyone else.

Now obviously the Word is for all of us. But God may put something on your heart that is just for you alone. He may say something like, "I don't want you eating sugar anymore," or, "You need to quit drinking caffeine," or, "I want you to stop drinking six soda pops a day." Has God ever said anything like that to you?

When the Lord speaks something like that to us, sometimes we think, *Oh, that's just an idea that I had, a thought that went through my head,* or we may know it is God speaking but don't really take it seriously. Perhaps we look at it as a suggestion, not a command. There really isn't any difference between divine suggestions and commands. Whatever God speaks to us is for our good, and we are being foolish if we don't listen and obey. Many times that is the reason we get into messes in our life — we don't pay attention to what God is telling us.

You may feel bad all the time simply because of something you are eating or drinking. God may know it, but you don't. You think it is okay because "everybody does it." So you just keep on doing it.

"Why not?" you say. "After all, I've done it all my life, and it's never bothered me before."

I came to the point a few years ago that I couldn't drink caffeine anymore. You have to understand, I used to brag about how I could drink a pot of coffee and go to bed and fall right to sleep. It was that way for a lot of years; caffeine just never bothered me.

Then all of a sudden, something changed in my mechanism; they call it hormones. When hormones get scrambled around, sometimes many other things get scrambled around with them.

Suddenly I was tired, more tired than usual. It seemed that stressful things bothered me more. Caffeine was putting stress on my body, and it was making me tense and keeping me from sleeping.

Another time I had been tired consistently for several months. I thought it was because I was traveling a lot and expected it to go away when I got a chance to rest. That opportunity did come and even though I rested, I was still tired. I asked the Lord one morning why I was so tired all the time, and I heard Him say in my heart, "You're eating too much food and overloading your body, and you're eating too much of the wrong kind of food."

When I got honest with myself and examined what I had been eating, I realized that the Lord was right, as He always is, and I made a change. The next day I felt better, and it continued. We always get good results when we obey the Lord.

My husband, Dave, had a similar experience. He could always drink caffeine with no problem, and then all of a sudden, he started getting what he called the "yips." He would get in bed at night, and he would have such a "buzz" that he couldn't go to sleep.

He started praying and asking God, "What is the problem?" and God told him (in his heart) — caffeine. Dave got off of caffeine, and he quit having the problem. To this day, if he eats too much chocolate — because chocolate has a lot of caffeine in it — he will get that same "buzz" at night and have trouble sleeping. Excessive sugar affects him the same way so he avoids it because feeling bad all the time makes life a lot harder.

Now Dave didn't have too much trouble because he listened to God. But it often happens that God tells a person something like what He told Dave, and they will spend the next twenty years feeling rotten because they don't want to do what God told them to do.

That's why we all have to be in personal obedience to God. Yet too often we will say something like, "Lord, I need You to heal my legs because they hurt all the time." So He says, "Change your eating habits and lose twenty pounds."

We become defensive and say, "But, Lord, my problem hasn't got anything to do with what I eat or what I weigh. I have been eating the same things and weighing the same amount for twenty years, and it has never bothered me before."

As we get older, we can't always do the same things we could do when we were younger. Actually, if we hadn't done some of those things when we were younger, we would probably feel better now that we are older.

When you are young, you think you can abuse your body and get by with it all your life. But it will catch up with you someday.

Many people's lives are a mess simply due to disobedience. Their disobedience may stem from ignorance or rebellion, but the only way out of the mess is repentance and a return to submission and obedience.

Submission Is an Action and an Attitude

Submit yourselves therefore to God. Resist the devil, and he will flee from you.

JAMES 4:7 KJV

I can't tell you how many years I heard only the second half of that Scripture quoted: *Resist the devil, and he will flee from you.* I never really paid any attention to the first half of that verse.

It is not going to do us one bit of good to try to resist the devil if we are not going to submit to God because the power to resist the devil is found in submitting to God.

If you want to keep Satan under your feet, you have got to walk in obedience. Don't have any known disobedience, any purposeful disobedience, in your life.

Do I ever disobey God? Yes. I don't plan to be disobedient, and I don't do it on purpose. I might lose my temper and say something that I shouldn't. But as soon as God starts dealing with me about it, as soon as He starts telling me, "You did wrong, and you had better get back in there and apologize and make it right," I do what He says.

I have a reverential fear of God[1] in my life, and I think we need a lot more of that. I believe that God is God, and I believe He means business. I believe that when He tells me to do something, He means it, and when He tells me not to do something, He means it.

Yes, we live under grace, but grace is not an excuse to sin; it is the power to live a holy life.

Extreme Obedience

Although He was a Son, He learned [active, special] obedience through what He suffered.

HEBREWS 5:8

The main reason people don't obey God is that it requires some suffering.

Anytime God wants you to do one thing, and your flesh wants to do something else, you are going to feel some pain if you follow God.

Let's look at some Scriptures on obedience and disobedience. Proverbs 11:3 says that contrariness and crookedness destroy people, and 1 Samuel 15:23 says that rebellion is like witchcraft and stubbornness is like idolatry.

Then notice what Philippians 2:8 says of Jesus: *And after He had appeared in human form, He abased and humbled Himself [still further] and carried His obedience to the extreme of death, even the death of the cross!*

Jesus was extremely obedient. He wasn't a little bit obedient. He wasn't partially obedient. He was fully and completely and extremely obedient.

I believe God loves to see people who will take their obedience to extremes. Are you one of them?

According to the Bible, the obedience of Jesus was so extreme that it cost Him His life. God is not asking us to get on a cross and shed our blood and die physically. But He is asking us to die to self.

Live Beyond Your Feelings

And Jesus called [to Him] the throng with His disciples and said to them, If anyone intends to come after Me, let him deny himself [forget, ignore, disown, and lose sight of himself and his own interests] and take up his cross, and [joining Me as a disciple and siding with My party] follow with Me [continually, cleaving steadfastly to Me].

MARK 8:34

Notice that *The Amplified Bible* translation of this Scripture says, . . . *forget, ignore, disown, and lose sight of himself and his own interests. . . .* So, really, the cross that we carry is not living a selfish, self-centered, "me, me, me" life but living a life that is willing to suffer to obey God.

Let me give you an example. Suppose I have $100 and plans for what I am going to do with it. Suppose somebody comes along, and God says to me, "You need to help that person by giving them the money." Or suppose somebody takes up an offering, and God tells me to put that $100 in the offering plate.

I might say, "But what about me, Lord? I have plans for that money."

If I am obedient to do what God says, there is going to be a little suffering because I will have to do without whatever I intended to buy with that money.

This kind of obedience is part of what Jesus means when He says that in order to follow Him we have to deny ourselves, or die to self. We must die to our own ways of being and doing — the fleshly ways of handling situations, and all its ways and demands. But it is that very obedience that gives us the power to overcome every adversity of the devil.

Jesus Ruled through Obedience

Therefore [because He stooped so low] God has highly exalted Him and has freely bestowed on Him the name that is above every name,

That in (at) the name of Jesus every knee should (must) bow, in heaven and on earth and under the earth.

PHILIPPIANS 2:9,10

The kingdom of darkness has no power over Jesus. Why? It is because He was extremely obedient.

Many times we like to use the name of Jesus like a magic charm by sticking it on the end of everything we want. But I don't really believe that His Name holds any real power for us unless we are walking in obedience to the best of our ability.

None of us in a human body is 100 percent obedient. I am not trying to put fear and guilt on anyone. I am talking about getting the junk out of our lives. I am talking about not just doing things because we think, *It doesn't matter what I do because God understands.*

For example, a woman who is living with her boyfriend or a man who is living with his girlfriend might try to excuse their behavior by saying, "Some people may think that what I'm doing is wrong, but God understands. After all, it's the twenty-first century."

It may be the twenty-first century, but it is still sin. It really doesn't matter what century it is, the Word of God is just as good in this century as it was ten centuries ago.

We've got to get over that kind of thinking — thinking that our society is so progressive now that we don't need the Word of God. All we have to do to disprove that notion is look at the results we are getting from all the open sin in the world today.

Today more than 50 percent of the people who get married don't stay married.[2] Teenagers are killing each other in school. They're shooting teachers if they get angry about something they don't like. Twenty or thirty years ago, the worst problem in school was chewing gum and throwing spit wads. Now it is drugs and violence.

We have progressed all right. We have come a long way all right. It is sad to say, but much of our progression has been downhill.

Now I know when I say things like this that I may be offending you because you may be living with someone outside of marriage or doing something else that God says not to do in His Word. I am not trying to offend you, hurt you or turn you off to the things of God. I am trying to help you. But I cannot help you if I just pat you on the head and tell you that whatever you want to do is okay because "God understands."

The door of disobedience is one of Satan's favorite entrances by which to gradually draw us into a web of sin that is devastating for us in the end. The Bible teaches us the importance of obeying the Word. Without that obedience, we will never enjoy authority over the devil.

The Word is the Word, and if God says something is wrong, it is wrong. If God says something is an abomination, it is an abomination.

Let God Lead Your Future

There shall not be found among you anyone who . . . uses divination, or is a soothsayer, or an augur, or a sorcerer,

Or a charmer, or a medium, or a wizard, or a necromancer.

For all who do these things are an abomination to the Lord. . . .

Deuteronomy 18:10-12

Today many people are going to fortune tellers and tarot card readers or calling psychics who charge them so much per minute to tell them their future. There are millions of people who follow the horoscope, basing their life on the stars. You may be one of them. But there is no need to worship the stars when you can worship the God Who made them.

The Bible has much to say about consulting with mediums and soothsayers and doing other kinds of activities that God considers an abomination.

"How do you know the Bible is true?" you may ask.

This Book has been attacked more than any other book in all of history, and it is still around. It is actually a compilation of sixty-six books all written by different authors, and yet it all coincides together and makes sense. That couldn't have just happened.

"Are there any mistakes in the Bible?"

I honestly don't know. There may be because of translation differences. It may be that every little jot and tittle is not exactly the way it is supposed to be, but I believe that God has preserved the integrity of His Word. I believe that we can live by what it says, and I don't just believe it because I decided to believe it. I believe it because it has been proven in my life.

Don't waste your money calling up people who supposedly can tell you about your future. Let God lead your future.

Remember that the Bible describes such things as horoscopes, tarot cards, psychic readings and fortune telling as an abomination unto God. But I think many people today don't even know those things are wrong. In fact, some churches don't even teach people that those things are wrong.

I went to a certain church before I was baptized in the Holy Spirit, and there was a woman in our church who was getting involved in transcendental meditation. Since she didn't know whether there was anything wrong with it or not, she went to our pastor and talked to him about it. He told her, "I'm not really sure. Let me know whether it works or not; I might even try it myself."

I didn't know any better then either. If God had not intervened in my life, I might have fallen into some of that kind of New Age activity.

There is no telling how many people are getting sucked into the New Age movement simply because they really don't know enough of the Word to know that they need to stay away from that kind of thing.

Listen to God

If any of you is deficient in wisdom, let him ask of the giving God [Who gives] to everyone liberally and ungrudgingly, without reproaching or fault-finding, and it will be given him.

JAMES 1:5

God will tell you everything you need to know if you will just listen to Him. Why in the world would you want to go to somebody else and ask what you should do with your life when their life is probably in a mess behind the scenes?

One psychiatrist told me, "I just counsel people with your tapes now." She said that after hearing me teach, she started meeting with her clients in private sessions and then sending them home with a set of my tapes.

This woman was serious. She told me, "I had all these people coming to me for counseling, and I thought, *I don't have a clue about what I'm telling these people; my life is in a worse mess than most of theirs.*

Then she said, "I got hold of your tapes and started listening to them, and finally decided to start giving them to my clients to listen to at home."

Now I am not saying there are no good psychiatrists or counselors, or that they are not helping people. But I am saying that if you go to somebody for counsel, you had better make sure it is somebody who is led by the Holy Spirit.

Matthew 15:14 says the blind cannot lead the blind; they will both fall into a ditch.

I surely wouldn't want some unsaved, worldly, New Age-type person trying to tell me how to handle my problems: "If you're angry, go into a room and beat a pillow. Work out that anger. Take it out on the pillow."

Instead of beating up your pillow, why not just try asking God for healing? Why not do what the Word says and forgive all those who have hurt you and made you angry? You might feel like beating up something once in a while — I felt that way for many years — but it doesn't do any good.

Learn to live beyond your feelings. Consult God first — for counsel, for help, for comfort, for guidance — and walk in obedience to His instructions to the best of your ability.

8

WALK IN LOVE

Way #5

And walk in love, [esteeming and delighting in one another] as Christ loved us and gave Himself up for us. . . .

EPHESIANS 5:2

You can defeat Satan with a good, strong, healthy love walk.

Not enough Christians concentrate on walking in love. We concentrate on prosperity. We concentrate on healing, success, our breakthrough, how to change our family, how to get our loved ones saved. But Jesus said:

I give you a new commandment: that you should love one another. Just as I have loved you, so you too should love one another.

By this shall all [men] know that you are My disciples, if you love one another [if you keep on showing love among yourselves].

John 13:34,35

If you want to be a witness for Christ, walk in love. To walk in love is to receive His love for you and allow it to flow to others.

A Sign of the Times

And the love of the great body of people will grow cold. . . .

Matthew 24:12

In Matthew chapter 24 Jesus was giving His disciples some of the signs of the end times: wars and rumors of wars, famines and earthquakes in many places, nations rising against nations.

In verse 12, Jesus said that as a sign of the end times *the love of the great body of people will grow* cold . . . . I believe that *the great body* of people is the church.

We have to be very sure that we don't get a stronghold of cold love in our life, a stronghold in which we have no compassion, a stronghold in which we do not really care about other people.

Let me ask you a question. Try to answer it honestly. Don't you feel that today, more than at any other time in your life, people really don't want to help other people?

Have you ever wondered why that is?

"I'd Rather Not Get Involved"

Then He poured water into the washbasin and began to wash the disciples' feet and to wipe them with the [servant's] towel with which He was girded.

When He came to Simon Peter, [Peter] said to Him, Lord, are my feet to be washed by You? [Is it for You to wash my feet?]

Jesus said to him, You do not understand now what I am doing, but you will understand later on.

Peter said to Him, You shall never wash my feet!
Jesus answered him, Unless I wash you, you have no
part with (in) Me [you have no share in compan-
ionship with Me].

JOHN 13:5-8

The number one reason we hear today for not helping others is, "I'd rather not get involved."

When Jesus tried to wash Peter's feet, Peter said, "No, You're not going to wash my feet!" And Jesus said to Peter, "If I don't wash you, you have no part in Me."

Do you know what I believe He was saying? As I mentioned earlier, I believe He was saying, "Help each other. Take care of each other. Do for one another. Meet each other's needs." I also believe He was saying, "If we don't get involved together here in meeting needs, then where is the companionship, the relationship, the unity between us?"

What kind of brotherhood do we have if we are not involved with one another? Yet we continue to hear people say, "I don't want to get involved. I'd rather not get involved. I got involved once, and I got hurt."

Everybody gets hurt. If you have been hurt in a relationship, go to God and allow Him to heal you; then get involved with people again.

Satan loves it when our love is cold toward one another and we don't get involved with others. It is actually an end-time, demonic warfare attack that gives Satan the upper hand over us. To keep him from gaining that advantage, we must develop and exercise a strong love walk — with God, with each other and with all those to whom God sends us.

Major in Love, Not Judgment

Do not judge and criticize and condemn others, so that you may not be judged and criticized and condemned yourselves.

For just as you judge and criticize and condemn others, you will be judged and criticized and condemned, and in accordance with the measure you [use to] deal out to others, it will be dealt out again to you.

> *Why do you stare from without at the very small particle that is in your brother's eye but do not become aware of and consider the beam of timber that is in your own eye?*
>
> MATTHEW 7:1-3

Judging people is a fruit of not loving people.

We need to major in the things that are major to God, and love is a major thing to Him.

One translation of Matthew 7:3 says, "Why are you trying to get the toothpick out of your brother's eye when you have a telephone pole in your own eye?"

Let's read what Jesus goes on to say in *The Amplified Bible* version of this passage:

> *Or how can you say to your brother, Let me get the tiny particle out of your eye, when there is the beam of timber in your own eye?*
>
> *You hypocrite, first get the beam of timber out of your own eye, and then you will see clearly to take the tiny particle out of your brother's eye.*
>
> MATTHEW 7:4,5

What is Jesus saying to us here? I believe He is saying, "You need to be concerned about what's wrong with you, not about what's wrong with everybody else."

That was true when Jesus first said it, and it is still true for us today. It is good advice to follow, especially since the fruit of judging people is an open door to Satan.

Judging Opens the Door to the Devil

Do not give that which is holy (the sacred thing) to the dogs, and do not throw your pearls before hogs, lest they trample upon them with their feet and turn and tear you in pieces.

MATTHEW 7:6

I have written in my Bible next to this Scripture that I believe that holy, sacred thing we have to give is love.

Now read between the lines. What is Jesus saying to us in this verse? I believe that He is saying, "When you judge people instead of loving them, the devil is going to have an open door in your life."

I believe that by judging and criticizing people, we open the door to Satan by casting the holy thing (love) before dogs and hogs (demon spirits). In Matthew 7:6, we saw the results: The dogs and hogs will turn around and attack us and tear us to pieces.

I wonder how much trouble we have in our lives because we open the door to Satan through judging other people: "I don't think they should be driving that kind of car. I don't think they should be doing this. I don't think they should be doing that. I don't think . . ."

May I share with you a piece of wisdom in this area? *Anywhere you don't have responsibility, don't bother to have an opinion.*

It's None of Our Business

> *. . . make it your ambition and definitely endeavor to live quietly and peacefully, to mind your own affairs, and to work with your hands, as we charged you.*

1 Thessalonians 4:11

This verse is a great scriptural instruction to mind our own business. For example, you don't have to worry about what I wear because you don't buy my clothes. Neither do I have to worry about what you wear because I don't buy your clothes. In other words, *judge not*.[1] Instead, show mercy because *Mercy triumphs over judgment*.[2]

We don't think enough about the right things, and we think too much about the wrong things. We like to get into other people's business. Yet the Bible clearly tells us to mind our own business and stay busy with our own hands if we want to have a good life.

Be a Blessing to Others

When angry, do not sin; do not ever let your wrath (your exasperation, your fury or indignation) last until the sun goes down.

Leave no [such] room or foothold for the devil [give no opportunity to him].

EPHESIANS 4:26,27

This passage tells us that when we get angry, we should not let the sun go down on our anger because if we do, we will open a door for the enemy. We will give him opportunities in our life. We will give him a foothold, and if we give him a foothold, then he may turn it into a stronghold.

The best way to keep the door closed to the enemy is to walk in love. People who walk in love don't stay mad because they are quick to forgive.

In 2 Corinthians 2:10,11, the apostle Paul instructed the people to forgive, saying:

If you forgive anyone anything, I too forgive that one; and what I have forgiven, if I have forgiven anything, has been for your sakes in the presence [and with the approval] of Christ (the Messiah),

To keep Satan from getting the advantage over us; for we are not ignorant of his wiles and intentions.

In Mark 11:25, Jesus tells us that when we pray, we are to forgive anybody we have anything against. If we don't do that in love, our faith won't work because, as Galatians 5:6 says, faith is activated, energized, expressed and worked through love.

How many people do you think are praying what they think is a prayer of faith, but they have no love walk?

What am I talking about when I say "a love walk"? I am talking about treating people better. I am talking about meeting needs. I am talking about how we talk *about* each other and how we talk *to* each other. I am talking about not being rude. I am talking about simple little things, such as standing in front of the tape table at a Christian conference and not shoving yourself in front of a bunch of people because you are in a hurry to buy the series on love!

That is just the way our flesh is: "I want to get my tapes so I can get my car out of the parking lot first because I'm in a hurry." Again, it's all about "me, me, me."

Walking in love means being a blessing to somebody else.

"What about Me?"

. . . Love (God's love in us) does not insist on its own rights or its own way, for it is not self-seeking. . . .

1 Corinthians 13:5

God has shown me a lot about selfishness because I used to be a very selfish, self-centered person. Oh, I prayed, I used the name of Jesus and rebuked devils, but I wasn't getting anything other than tired. I didn't understand what was wrong because I was doing everything I had been told to do to get my prayers answered.

Do you ever feel that way? "I'm so tired. God, I'm so tired of all this. I'm doing everything I should, but nothing is happening. I don't understand what's wrong."

The reason nothing is happening may be that you are doing the wrong things. You are doing, but you are trying to do what only God can do. You are so busy doing the wrong things that you never pay any attention to doing the right things.

I had much to learn about selfishness, and one morning God gave me a revelation on it.

That morning I woke up and was lying in bed thinking about myself. Do you ever do that? Do you ever lie in bed and just think about yourself, not only about your problems but about how you can get everybody to bless you?

As I was doing that, God said to me (in my heart), "You know, you all remind me of a bunch of robots. As soon as you wake up in the morning, it is as though the devil runs over and winds up this metal key in your back nice and tight."

Isn't that the truth? If we lie in bed and think about ourselves, what we are really doing is getting ourselves all wound up for the day because where the mind goes, the man follows. As the Bible says, as we think in our heart, so are we.[3]

God said to me that morning, "You are all like a bunch of mechanical robots. The enemy winds you up, and this is what I hear all day: 'What about me?

What about me? What about me — me, me, me, me? What about me?"'

When I tell this story in my meetings, I often walk like a robot, an imitation that has become very popular with my audiences. In fact, they are always saying to me, "Joyce, do the robot. Do the robot."

Over the years, people who have seen me do my robot imitation have sent me a few toy robots. One of them carries a banner that reads, "What about me? What about me?"

It is impossible to overcome adversity while leading a selfish lifestyle. Remember, one of the first things the Bible says about love is that it is not selfish or self-seeking. Love does not do the right thing to get something; love simply does the right thing because it is the right thing to do.

Walking in love may mean living in a new way, but it is worth the effort. It not only blesses others; it blesses the one doing the loving.

9

KNOW THE DIFFERENCE BETWEEN YOUR "WHO" AND YOUR "DO"

Way #6

Stand therefore, having girded your waist with truth, having put on the breastplate of righteousness.

EPHESIANS 6:14 NKJV

One of the pieces of spiritual armor that we are told to put on in Ephesians chapter 6 is the breastplate of righteousness. *The Living Bible* calls it *the breastplate of God's approval.*

You need to know that God loves you, that you have been made the righteousness of God in His

Son Jesus Christ.[1] No one knows you as well as God does. Yet, even though He knows everything about you, including your faults, He still approves of you and accepts you, as He does all of us. Now He does not approve of our wrong behavior, but He still loves us.

In this chapter, you will have an opportunity to learn the difference between your "who" and your "do." Let me explain what I mean.

You may not do everything right, but God sees your heart. If you want to do right, if you want to obey God, but you just don't have enough knowledge yet or you still need some training, God understands that. He will never stop working with you to help you change into the person He created you to be.

In 2 Corinthians 3:18 KJV, the Bible says that we go from glory to glory, but we don't just change overnight. God understands where we came from. He understands the backgrounds out of which we came. He understands the things that were done to us, the misconceptions we have of ourselves — and

He works with us to overcome all that. He helps us defeat our enemies little by little.[2]

In the meantime, 2 Corinthians 5:17 KJV tells us that if any person is in Christ, he is a new creature; old things have passed away, all things have become new. Verse 21 of that passage says that Jesus, Who knew no sin, became sin so that we could be made the righteousness of God in Him.

So that is who you are. Now that you are in Christ, you are the righteousness of God in Him. You don't always *do* everything right, but that doesn't change *who* you are.

My children don't always do everything I want them to, but they are still my children, and I still love them. I don't want a neighbor, friend or enemy telling me what's wrong with my kids because they are my kids, and I will take care of them.

So when the devil tells you everything you are doing wrong, you ought to say to him, "Thank you for reminding me, but let me remind you that I am still the righteousness of God in Christ Jesus, and I am being changed from glory to glory. I am not perfect, but I am acceptable to God because of what Jesus has already done for me. Jesus was made perfect for me. My right standing with God is not based on my performance, but on my faith and trust in Jesus' performance."

Understanding Righteousness

Blessed be the God and Father of our Lord Jesus Christ, who has blessed us with every spiritual blessing in the heavenly places in Christ,

just as He chose us in Him before the foundation of the world, that we should be holy and without blame before Him in love,

having predestined us to adoption as sons by Jesus Christ to Himself, according to the good pleasure of His will,

to the praise of the glory of His grace, by which He has made us accepted in the Beloved.

EPHESIANS 1:3-6 NKJV

In order to know who you are in Jesus Christ, you have to fully understand righteousness. You are not going to do that in the short time it takes to read this book.

Grasping the understanding of godly righteousness is probably one of the most difficult things for us to get through our legalistic, rigid, religion-soaked minds. I know because I remember what a hard time I had grasping it.

Why is it so hard for us to understand that we who are in Christ Jesus have already been made the righteousness of God, that we are already acceptable to Him just as we are? It is because the world teaches us that we are accepted based on what we do. That is self-righteousness, which is earned through right actions.

We only have that kind of righteousness if we do everything perfectly. When we make a mistake, we no longer have it, and we feel bad about losing it. God's righteousness is quite the opposite; it is not earned by us but is freely given to us by the Lord.

According to the Bible, we are made acceptable in the Beloved. That means that if we believe in

Jesus, we will never be rejected or condemned. God's righteousness is given to us by grace through faith in His Son Jesus.[3] It is not based on what we do but on what we believe — or more precisely in Whom we believe.

Your "Who" Will Fix Your "Do"

He who believes in Him [who clings to, trusts in, relies on Him] is not judged [he who trusts in Him never comes up for judgment; for him there is no rejection, no condemnation — he incurs no damnation]; but he who does not believe (cleave to, rely on, trust in Him) is judged already [he has already been convicted and has already received his sentence] because he has not believed in and trusted in the name of the only begotten Son of God. [He is condemned for refusing to let his trust rest in Christ's name].

JOHN 3:18

This is such a good Scripture. It tells us that what God is looking for in us is Who we believe in, not what we do.

I believe Jesus died for my sins. I believe that although I am imperfect, my heart is right toward God. I love Him as much as I know how. I believe I am changing every day, but I know I am not perfected yet. I believe that the blood of Jesus washes away my sins. I repent of my sins, and I believe that I walk in continual forgiveness[4] because every time God points out a sin to me, I sincerely repent of it. I believe that the blood — not my performance, but the blood of Jesus Christ — has made me right with God. Therefore, I believe that I am not judged.

That doesn't mean I don't need to change. It doesn't mean I don't need to improve. It just means I know the difference between my "who" and my "do."

Do you know the difference between your "who" and your "do"? If not, you are going to feel guilty about something all the time because you are always going to be trying to change and improve. But it isn't going to work, and you're going to feel that you have not done everything God requires you to do to be acceptable and pleasing to Him.

If you are trying to "do" so your "who" will be right, that isn't what God requires. God is concerned with our motives. He doesn't want us to do things to make up for what we have done wrong or to be acceptable to Him. There is only one kind of "do" that makes us acceptable to Him, and that is to believe, to have faith in what Jesus has done, not faith in what we can do.

I encourage you to say every day, "I'm putting my dependence on who I am in Christ, rather than on what I do for Him, and He is helping me to do right things for right reasons."

10

THINK ABOUT WHAT YOU ARE THINKING ABOUT

Way #7

. . . whatever is true, whatever is worthy of reverence and is honorable and seemly, whatever is just, whatever is pure, whatever is lovely and lovable, whatever is kind and winsome and gracious, if there is any virtue and excellence, if there is anything worthy of praise, think on and weigh and take account of these things [fix your minds on them].

PHILIPPIANS 4:8

You have probably heard lots of good teaching on the mind so I am not going to go into great detail here. But if you will read this one passage of Scripture prayerfully, I think you will see the point: You need to be careful about your thoughts. You need to think about what you are thinking about.

When you start feeling discouraged and depressed, if you will stop and take an inventory of your thoughts, many times you will discover why you are feeling that way.

As we saw previously, 2 Corinthians 10:4 tells us that God has given us spiritual weapons to tear down strongholds in our life. Negative thinking is a stronghold of the mind that our spiritual weapons can tear down. As we will see next, the mind is where the battle with the enemy actually takes place.

The Mind Is the Battlefield

[Inasmuch as we] refute arguments and theories and reasonings and every proud and lofty thing that sets itself up against the [true] knowledge of God; and we lead every thought and purpose away

captive into the obedience of Christ (the Messiah, the Anointed One). . . .

2 CORINTHIANS 10:5

The mind is the battlefield. That is the place where Satan does war with us.

When Satan attacked Jesus in the wilderness with temptations, and the Bible says, . . . *the devil said to Him [Jesus] . . . ,*[1] I believe those temptations came to Jesus' mind as thoughts. We have already seen how Jesus handled those thoughts. He refuted them by quoting the Word of God.

Second Corinthians 10:5 tells us that we are to do the same thing as Jesus. We are to refute all *arguments and theories and reasonings and every proud and lofty thing that sets itself up against the [true] knowledge of God.* We are to *lead every thought and purpose away captive into the obedience of Christ.* We are to use the weapon of the Word and continue to use it to defeat the devil and keep him under our feet.

The Word Destroys Mental Strongholds

For the Word that God speaks is alive and full of power [making it active, operative, energizing, and

effective]; it is sharper than any two-edged sword,
penetrating to the dividing line of the breath of life
(soul) and [the immortal] spirit, and of joints and
marrow [of the deepest parts of our nature], expos-
ing and sifting and analyzing and judging the very
thoughts and purposes of the heart.

HEBREWS 4:12

If you are not familiar with these Scriptures, you
need to study them and meditate on them. What
they are basically saying is that we have weapons.
The Word of God is one of those key weapons.
Prayer is another weapon. Spending time with God
is another weapon. Walking in love is a weapon.
Watching our words is a weapon.

With one of those weapons, the Word of God,
we can bring down mental strongholds.

For example, I had to learn to use God's Word to
break down a stronghold the devil had in my
mind. I thought for years that because I had been
sexually abused in my childhood I was so messed
up that I could never be any good, that nobody

would ever want me. I believed those things because that is what Satan told me.

When I got in the Word, I started discovering the truth. I saw that the Bible says that God would give me a double reward for my former shame.[2] I found out I could have double for my trouble if I followed God.

I had a stronghold in my life, the thought that I was no good. Then I began to get some truth down inside me. Now when those negative thoughts arise, the spirit within me rises up and wields the two-edged sword of the Word against the lies of Satan.

I use my mouth to speak forth that truth: "No, Satan, I am good in God. I am not good in myself, but His goodness dwells in me, and He has a good plan for my life. I have overcome my past because I have let go of what lies behind and am pressing on to the good things that lie ahead."

Speaking forth the truth to the devil like that is the only way to see a mindset changed.

If you have some kind of mental stronghold, I believe God is talking directly to you through this book. This is the time to bring those thoughts into line with the Word and press on toward the good things He has in store for you. The choice is yours. If you will do this and dare to believe that God will change things, it will only be a matter of time until He does.

11

PRAY AT ALL TIMES

Way #8

Pray at all times (on every occasion, in every season) in the Spirit, with all [manner of] prayer and entreaty. To that end keep alert and watch with strong purpose and perseverance, interceding in behalf of all the saints (God's consecrated people).

EPHESIANS 6:18

This verse actually describes the last piece of spiritual armor presented in Ephesians chapter 6 — prayer. Prayer is simply conversation with God; it is our request, our petition. Basically, in this verse the apostle Paul was telling us, "When you need something, ask God for it."

Paul also talked about prayer in Philippians 4:6 NKJV, saying, *Be anxious for nothing, but in everything by prayer and supplication, with thanksgiving, let your requests be made known to God.* In other words, pray, tell God your need and be thankful.

Offering up to God the prayer of thanksgiving, the prayer of worship and the prayer of praise is another part of prayer. In the Old Testament, the psalmist said of God, *Seven times a day and all day long do I praise You because of Your righteous decrees.*[1] In the New Testament, Paul wrote, *I desire therefore that in every place men should pray, without anger or quarreling or resentment or doubt [in their minds], lifting up holy hands.*[2]

One time I read this verse in my hotel room before a meeting, and I just lifted up my hands and starting praying, "God, I love You. I worship You, Lord. I magnify Your name." Then I said, "Help me to remember to do that seven times a day."

Praise and worship confuse the enemy. If you are not already doing so, make a point to stop occasionally throughout the day and give praise to God, and you will see the devil's defeat.

Take a Praise Pause

He who brings an offering of praise and thanksgiving honors and glorifies Me. . . .

PSALM 50:23

We need to take praise pauses. During the day we need to pause and say, "Thank You, Lord. I love You. You are worthy to be praised."

To remind yourself to do this at home, I suggest putting a sign up in your house that says, "Take a Praise Pause."

I sincerely believe that if you will start doing more praying, praising and worshipping God, if you will start spending more time being thankful to Him, and get over complaining and murmuring, you will begin to see some changes in your life.

Intercede in Prayer

First of all, then, I admonish and urge that petitions, prayers, intercessions, and thanksgivings be offered on behalf of all men. . . .

For such [praying] is good and right, and [it is]
pleasing and acceptable to God our Savior.
1 TIMOTHY 2:1,3

Intercede for other people. To intercede is to
stand in the gap for someone else, to plead their
case to God. Praying for others is like sowing seed.
If you sow a seed, you will reap a harvest.[3] When
you sow into somebody else's life, God meets your
needs. So by praying for people, you reap a harvest
of blessings in your own life as well.

You may also need to pray for yourself that you
come not into temptation. As Jesus told us in
Matthew 26:41, *All of you must keep awake (give*
strict attention, be cautious and active) and watch
and pray, that you may not come into temptation.
The spirit indeed is willing, but the flesh is weak.

This kind of prayer is especially important if
there are areas in your life that you know are real
areas of temptation for you.

If you know you are going to be around a certain
person who always makes you mad, don't just hope

that individual doesn't upset you. Don't just try not to get mad the next time you meet that individual. Spend some time in prayer before you come into contact with that person. Say, "Lord, I need You to strengthen me because every time I get around this person, I end up getting mad, and I don't want to fall into that temptation. Help me, Lord."

If you pray ahead of time, you will be better prepared to face that temptation.

The same is true for other problem areas. If you are tempted in your appetite, for example, then pray about it before you sit down at the table. Don't just bless your food and gobble it down. Before you even start to eat, say, "Lord, You have got to help me. Help me to make right choices here. Help me to choose things that are going to be good for me and healthy for my body."

Do the praying and let God do the working. Prayer is one way to have power over the devil.

Pray Your Way through the Day

. . . The earnest (heartfelt, continued) prayer of a righteous man makes tremendous power available [dynamic in its working].

JAMES 5:16

If you want to have power against Satan, you need to learn how to pray your way through the day.

Prayer is one of the ways we believers have spiritual authority over the enemy. It is a very definite privilege and advantage because the act of prayer binds evil, looses good[4] and brings about action that will cause change in a situation.

Pray about everything; pray about anything. Pray in the grocery store. Pray in the car. Pray in the house. Pray in the church. Pray silently. Pray out loud. Pray in agreement[5] — but pray at all times.

God can work out things for our good that Satan intends for our harm[6] when we pray. So pray everywhere, in every season and on every occasion, and you will be more than the devil can handle. You will defeat him every time — and he hates that!

Conclusion

In this book, I have shared some of the things the Lord has taught me over the years on overcoming adversity.

As I have mentioned, our value is not in what we do but in who we are in Christ. Always walk in love. The devil doesn't know what to do with a person who is willing to put others before themselves as a service to God. Pray at all times because prayer opens the windows of heaven and closes the gates of hell. It is the difference between victory and defeat.

Be careful what you think because the mind is the battlefield where Satan most often attacks you. Don't believe everything that comes into your mind. Cast down wrong thoughts that don't agree with

God's Word. Always keep in mind that . . . *greater is he that is in you, than he that is in the world.*[1]

Obedience is one of the most important keys to overcoming adversity. The devil cannot defeat an obedient believer who has firmly placed their trust in God.

I believe this message contains rich and powerful truths that will help you learn to manage adversity instead of letting adversity manage you. I pray that you will not only meditate upon it but that you will put it into practice. If you will dig in your heels and determine that Satan is not going to get his way, it won't take long for you to begin to see radical changes in virtually every area of your life.

The devil wants you to be hopeless, depressed, discouraged, lukewarm, cold and apathetic. He wants you to be an easy target for his attacks. By aggressively standing against him, you will strip him of his power, shut the door on him and open the door to his defeat.

PRAYER FOR
OVERCOMING ADVERSITY

Pray this prayer out loud:

Father, I thank You that because Your Son Jesus died on the cross and defeated Satan, I have power and authority over the enemy. Right now I am going to begin to exercise that power and authority and put him in his rightful place, which is under my feet.

In the name of Jesus, I declare that by God's grace I will no longer allow Satan to steal the Word from me. I will put on the shoes of peace so that I may remain peaceful at all times. I will spend time with You and in Your Word, being careful to watch my mouth and to submit myself to You in personal obedience. I will walk in love, knowing the difference between who I am in Christ Jesus and what I do in my human frailty, thinking about what I am think-ing about and praying at all times and in all places about everything. Thank You for Your love for me and for Your glorious plan for my life. In Jesus' name I pray, amen.

Scriptures to Confess to Overcome Adversity

It would be ridiculous for God to tell us that we can overcome adversity and not give us the means to accomplish the task. That is why God has given us His Word — to *use it.*

I highly recommend speaking the Word out of your mouth because as we have seen, the Word is the two-edged sword that must be wielded against the enemy. Confess the following Scriptures as often as you need to, and counter the devil's attack with the same weapon that Jesus used: *the Word!*

Behold, I have set the land before you; go in and take possession of the land which the Lord swore to your fathers, to Abraham, to Isaac, and to Jacob, to give to them and to their descendants after them.

DEUTERONOMY 1:8

Every place upon which the sole of your foot shall tread, that have I given to you, as I promised Moses.

JOSHUA 1:3

This Book of the Law shall not depart out of your mouth, but you shall meditate on it day and night, that you may observe and do according to all that is written in it. For then you shall make your way prosperous, and then you shall deal wisely and have good success.

JOSHUA 1:8

And all these blessings shall come upon you and overtake you if you heed the voice of the Lord your God.

DEUTERONOMY 28:2

Arise [from the depression and prostration in which circumstances have kept you — rise to a new life]! Shine (be radiant with the glory of the Lord), for your light has come, and the glory of the Lord has risen upon you!

ISAIAH 60:1

But be doers of the Word [obey the message], and not merely listeners to it, betraying yourselves [into deception by reasoning contrary to the Truth].

JAMES 1:22

Finally, my brethren, be strong in the Lord and in the power of His might.

Put on the whole armor of God, that you may be able to stand against the wiles of the devil.

For we do not wrestle against flesh and blood, but against principalities, against powers, against the rulers of the darkness of this age, against spiritual hosts of wickedness in the heavenly places.

Therefore take up the whole armor of God, that you may be able to withstand in the evil day, and having done all, to stand.

Stand therefore, having girded your waist with truth, having put on the breastplate of righteousness,

and having shod your feet with the preparation of the gospel of peace;

above all, taking the shield of faith with which you will be able to quench all the fiery darts of the wicked one.

And take the helmet of salvation, and the sword of the Spirit, which is the word of God.

EPHESIANS 6:10-17 NKJV

And do not [for a moment] be frightened or intimidated in anything by your opponents and adversaries, for such [constancy and fearlessness] will be a clear sign (proof and seal) to them of [their impending] destruction, but [a sure token and evidence] of your deliverance and salvation, and that from God.

PHILIPPIANS 1:28

But no weapon that is formed against you shall prosper, and every tongue that shall rise against you in judgment you shall show to be in the wrong. This [peace, righteousness, security, triumph over opposition] is the heritage of the servants of the Lord. . . .

ISAIAH 54:17

For thus said the Lord God, the Holy One of Israel: In returning [to Me] and resting [in Me] you shall be saved; in quietness and in [trusting] confidence shall be your strength. . . .

ISAIAH 30:15

He who dwells in the secret place of the Most High shall remain stable and fixed under the shadow of the Almighty [Whose power no foe can withstand].

PSALM 91:1

Submit yourselves therefore to God. Resist the devil, and he will flee from you.

JAMES 4:7 KJV

Leave no [such] room or foothold for the devil [give no opportunity to him].

EPHESIANS 4:27

If you forgive anyone anything, I [Paul] too forgive that one; and what I have forgiven, if I have forgiven anything, has been for your sakes in the presence [and with the approval] of Christ (the Messiah),

To keep Satan from getting the advantage over us; for we are not ignorant of his wiles and intentions.

2 CORINTHIANS 2:10,11

For the weapons of our warfare are not physical [weapons of flesh and blood], but they are mighty before God for the overthrow and destruction of strongholds,

[Inasmuch as we] refute arguments and theories and reasonings and every proud and lofty thing that sets itself up against the [true] knowledge of God; and we lead every thought and purpose away captive into the obedience of Christ (the Messiah, the Anointed One).

2 CORINTHIANS 10:4,5

For the Word that God speaks is alive and full of power [making it active, operative, energizing, and effective]; it is sharper than any two-edged sword, penetrating to the dividing line of the breath of life (soul) and [the immortal] spirit, and of joints and marrow [of the deepest parts of our nature], exposing and sifting and analyzing and judging the very thoughts and purposes of the heart.

HEBREWS 4:12

Pray at all times (on every occasion, in every season) in the Spirit, with all [manner of] prayer and entreaty. To that end keep alert and watch with strong purpose and perseverance, interceding in behalf of all the saints (God's consecrated people).

EPHESIANS 6:18

For such [praying] is good and right, and [it is] pleasing and acceptable to God our Savior.

1 TIMOTHY 2:3

. . . The earnest (heartfelt, continued) prayer of a righteous man makes tremendous power available [dynamic in its working].

JAMES 5:16

Prayer for a Personal
Relationship with the Lord

God wants you to receive His free gift of salvation. Jesus wants to save you and fill you with the Holy Spirit more than anything. If you have never invited Jesus, the Prince of Peace, to be your Lord and Savior, I invite you to do so now. Pray the following prayer, and if you are really sincere about it, you will experience a new life in Christ.

Father,

You loved the world so much, You gave Your only begotten Son to die for our sins so that whoever believes in Him will not perish, but have eternal life.

Your Word says we are saved by grace through faith as a gift from You. There is nothing we can do to earn salvation.

I believe and confess with my mouth that Jesus Christ is Your Son, the Savior of the world. I believe He died on the cross for me and bore all of my sins, paying the price for them. I believe in my heart that You raised Jesus from the dead.

I ask You to forgive my sins. I confess Jesus as my Lord. According to Your Word, I am saved and will spend eternity with You! Thank You, Father. I am so grateful! In Jesus' name, amen.

See John 3:16; Ephesians 2:8,9; Romans 10:9,10; 1 Corinthians 15:3,4; 1 John 1:9; 4:14-16; 5:1,12,13.

ENDNOTES

Introduction

1. See Genesis 1:27,28.
2. See Genesis chapter 3.
3. John 10:10; 8:44.
4. See Revelation 20:3.
5. See Luke 10:19.
6. See Romans 14:17.

Part 1 It's All About Doing

Chapter 1

1. See Exodus 12:31,40.
2. See Numbers 33:48,49.
3. See Numbers 33:53.
4. See Romans 5:6-11.
5. See Ephesians 6:12.
6. See Romans 8:13.
7. 1 Corinthians 15:31.

Chapter 2

1. Hebrews 13:8.
2. Philippians 4:13 KJV.
3. See Ephesians 5:22; Colossians 3:18.
4. See Colossians 3:5,8-10.
5. See Genesis 17:9-14.
6. Romans 2:28,29.
7. Galatians 5:22,23 KJV.

Chapter 3

[1] See Malachi 3:8.

[2] See Psalm 31:15.

[3] Mark 9:34.

[4] Everything we are and need — our redemption, our completeness, our wisdom, strength, peace, and hope — is found "in Christ." See Colossians 2:10.

[5] John 13:15.

[6] John 13:17.

[7] See Psalm 44:5; Luke 9:1.

[8] See James 4:7.

Part 2 Eight Ways to Overcome Adversity

Introduction

[1] See John 8:32.

Chapter 4

[1] See John 8:58.

[2] See 1 Corinthians 12:4-11.

[3] See Hebrews 1:3; 8:1; 12:2; Revelation 3:21.

[4] Hebrew 10:12,13.

[5] See Hebrews 9:1-7.

[6] See Exodus 28:33-35.

[7] Hebrews 9:11-28.

Chapter 5

[1] "According to many investigators the ark was originally a war sanctuary. . . . That the ark was designed to be a symbol of the presence of God in the midst of His people is the common teaching of the Old Testament." *International Standard Bible*

Encyclopedia, Original James Orr 1915 Edition, Electronic Database (copyright © 1995-1996 by Biblesoft), "Ark of the Covenant." All rights reserved.

2   See Mark 16:19.

Chapter 6

1   John 6:63.

2   Isaiah 61:3 KJV.

3   Psalm 42:5.

4   Romans 4:17 KJV.

5   Romans 4:17.

6   John 8:44.

7   Luke 3:22.

8   See Romans 3:22; 2 Corinthians 5:21.

9   2 Corinthians 10:4 KJV.

10   See Psalm 118:17.

11   See Numbers 32:11,12.

12   See 1 Corinthians 10:5-8.

13   Psalm 141:3.

14   Ezekiel 37:10.

Chapter 7

1   "The fear of the Lord signifies that religious reverence which every intelligent being owes to his Creator. . . ." *Clarke's Commentary,* by Adam Clarke, Electronic Database (copyright © 1996 by Biblesoft), "Proverbs 1:7." All rights reserved.

2   Based on information that estimates that 50 percent of first marriages now end in divorce. Debra Baker, "Beyond Ozzie and Harriet," *ABA*

Journal, (Chicago: Copyright American Bar Association, September 1998).

Chapter 8

[1] Matthew 7:1 KJV.

[2] James 2:13 NKJV.

[3] Proverbs 23:7 KJV.

Chapter 9

[1] 2 Corinthians 5:21.

[2] See Exodus 23:30.

[3] Grace is the power of God available to meet our needs. It is received by believing rather than through human effort.

[4] See 1 John 1:7.

Chapter 10

[1] Luke 4:1-13.

[2] See Isaiah 61:7.

Chapter 11

[1] Psalm 119:164.

[2] 1 Timothy 2:8.

[3] See Galatians 6:7.

[4] See Matthew 16:19.

[5] See Matthew 18:19.

[6] See Genesis 50:20.

Conclusion

[1] 1 John 4:4 KJV.

About the Author

Joyce Meyer has been teaching the Word of God since 1976 and in full-time ministry since 1980. Previously the associate pastor at Life Christian Church in St. Louis, Missouri, she developed, coordinated, and taught a weekly meeting known as "Life In The Word." After more than five years, the Lord brought it to a conclusion, directing her to establish her own ministry and call it *"Life In The Word, Inc."*

Now, her *Life In The Word* radio and television broadcasts are seen and heard by millions across the United States and throughout the world. Joyce's teaching tapes are enjoyed internationally, and she travels extensively conducting *Life In The Word* conferences.

Joyce and her husband, Dave, the business administrator at *Life In The Word,* have been married for over 35 years. They reside in St. Louis, Missouri, and are the parents of four children. All four children are married and, along with their spouses, work with Dave and Joyce in the ministry.

Believing the call on her life is to establish believers in God's Word, Joyce says, "Jesus died to set the captives free, and far too many Christians have little or no victory in their daily lives." Finding herself in the same situation many years ago and having found freedom to live in victory through applying God's Word, Joyce goes equipped to set captives free and to exchange ashes for beauty. She believes that every person who walks in victory leads many others into victory. Her life is transparent, and her teachings are practical and can be applied in everyday life.

Joyce has taught on emotional healing and related subjects in meetings all over the country, helping multiplied thousands. She has recorded more than 230 different audiocassette albums and over 75 videos. She has also authored 51 books to help the body of Christ on various topics.

Her "Emotional Healing Package" contains over 23 hours of teaching on the subject. Albums included in this package are: "Confidence"; "Beauty for Ashes" (includes Joyce's teaching notes); "Managing Your Emotions"; "Bitterness, Resentment, and Unforgiveness"; "Root of Rejection"; and a 90-minute Scripture/music tape titled "Healing the Brokenhearted."

Joyce's "Mind Package" features five different audio tape series on the subject of the mind. They include: "Mental Strongholds and Mindsets"; "Wilderness Mentality"; "The Mind of the Flesh"; "The Wandering, Wondering Mind"; and "Mind, Mouth, Moods, and Attitudes." The package also contains Joyce's powerful book, *Battlefield of the Mind.* On the subject of love she has three tape series titled "Love Is..."; "Love: The Ultimate Power"; and "Loving God, Loving Yourself, and Loving Others," and a book titled *Reduce Me to Love.*

Write to Joyce Meyer's office for a resource catalog and further information on how to obtain the tapes you need to bring total healing to your life.

To contact the author write:
Joyce Meyer Ministries
P. O. Box 655
Fenton, Missouri 63026
or call: (636) 349-0303

Internet Address: www.joycemeyer.org

Please include your testimony or help received from this book when you write. Your prayer requests are welcome.

To contact the author
in Canada, please write:
Joyce Meyer Ministries Canada, Inc.
Lambeth Box 1300
London, ON N6P 1T5
or call: (636) 349-0303

In Australia, please write:
Joyce Meyer Ministries-Australia
Locked Bag 77
Mansfield Delivery Centre
Queensland 4122
or call: 07 3349 1200

In England, please write:
Joyce Meyer Ministries
P. O. Box 1549
Windsor
SL4 1GT
or call: (0) 1753-831102

Books by Joyce Meyer

Secrets to Exceptional Living

Eight Ways to Overcome Adversity

Teenagers Are People Too!

Filled with the Spirit

A Celebration of Simplicity

The Joy of Believing Prayer

Never Lose Heart

Being the Person God Made You to Be

A Leader in the Making

"Good Morning, This Is God!" Gift Book

JESUS — Name Above All Names

"Good Morning, This Is God!" Daily Calendar

Help Me — I'm Married!

Reduce Me to Love

Be Healed in Jesus' Name

How to Succeed at Being Yourself

Eat and Stay Thin

Weary Warriors, Fainting Saints

Life in the Word Journal

Life in the Word Devotional

Be Anxious for Nothing

Be Anxious for Nothing Study Guide

The Help Me! Series:
I'm Alone!
I'm Stressed! • I'm Insecure!
I'm Discouraged! • I'm Depressed!
I'm Worried! • I'm Afraid!

Don't Dread

Managing Your Emotions

Healing the Brokenhearted

"Me and My Big Mouth!"

"Me and My Big Mouth!" Study Guide

Prepare to Prosper

Do It! Afraid

Expect a Move of God in Your Life . . . **Suddenly**

Enjoying Where You Are on the Way to Where You Are Going

The Most Important Decision You'll Ever Make

When, God, When?

Why, God, Why?

The Word, the Name, the Blood

Battlefield of the Mind

Battlefield of the Mind Study Guide

Tell Them I Love Them

Peace

The Root of Rejection

Beauty for Ashes

If Not for the Grace of God

New: If Not for the Grace of God Study Guide

By Dave Meyer
Nuggets of Life

Available from your local bookstore.

Harrison House
Tulsa, Oklahoma 74153

www.harrisonhouse.com

The Harrison House Vision

Proclaiming the truth and the power

Of the Gospel of Jesus Christ

With excellence;

Challenging Christians to

Live victoriously,

Grow spiritually,

Know God intimately.